The
Jews for Jesus
Family Cookbook

A Purple Pomegranate Book
San Francisco, California

The Jews for Jesus Family Cookbook © 1994
by Purple Pomegranate Productions
84 Page Street, San Francisco, CA 94102

Second Edition © 2005
All rights reserved. For reprint permission, please write to Purple Pomegranate
Productions, Permissions Department, 84 Page Street, San Francisco, CA 94102

Cover design by David Yapp
Inside design and layout by Susan Logsdon

ISBN   1-881-022-03-x

Moskowitz, Melissa, 1951-
       The Jews for Jesus Family Cookbook/by Melissa Moskowitz.—2nd ed.

       1. Cooking
       2. Jewish Culture
1. Title.

Purple Pomegranate Productions is a division of Jews for Jesus,
60 Haight Street, San Francisco, California 94102 • www.jewsforjesus.org

Contents

Psalm 128:2   You will eat the fruit of your labor; blessings and prosperity will be yours.

Genesis 1:29,30   Then God said, "I give you every seed-bearing plant on the face of the whole earth and every tree that has fruit with seed in it. They will be yours for food. And to all the beasts of the earth and all the birds of the air and all the creatures that move on the ground—everything that has the breath of life in it—I give every green plant for food." And it was so.

Psalm 104:14   He makes grass grow for the cattle, and plants for man to cultivate—bringing forth food from the earth:

Psalm 104:27   These all look to you to give them their food at the proper time.

Psalm 111:5   He provides food for those who fear him; he remembers his covenant forever.

Psalm 132:15   I will bless her with abundant provisions; her poor will I satisfy with food.

Acts 14:17   Yet he has not left himself without testimony: He has shown kindness by giving you rain from heaven and crops in their seasons; he provides you with plenty of food and fills your hearts with joy.

1 Timothy 6:8   But if we have food and clothing, we will be content with that.

Ecclesiastes 2:24   A man can do nothing better than to eat and drink and find satisfaction in his work. This too, I see, is from the hand of God,

1 Corinthians 10:31   So whether you eat or drink or whatever you do, do it all for the glory of God.

Foreword

This book of recipes is a labor of love and a statement of domesticity. Melissa Moskowitz began writing it in 1981 and includes recipes taken with the Moskowitz's to three different states as they moved here and there. Melissa loves to entertain, and she loves to write. She also loves to tell people about Jesus. Oh, did I mention that she loves to eat, too?! Of course, that goes without saying, but the fact that she has managed to keep slim is impressive. . .she weighs no more than she did when she married Jhan on August 2, 1976. This is after having two daughters, collecting about 325 recipes, traveling around this world far enough to have reached the moon, battling a serious bout of viral encephalitis, and getting a graduate degree in missiology. This recipe book grew along with the Moskowitz family in experience, spiritual maturity and a continuing love for people and the Lord.

Melissa is still looking for recipes. She finds them interesting, and sometimes even useful, but she has this to say when it comes to cooking: "From now on, I'm getting take-out." We can only hope that some of the restaurants from which she takes out will use her recipes. Melissa agrees that fasting is more spiritual than eating and that prayer is more profitable than indulgence, but she offers these recipes for your enjoyment. After all, Scripture does say, "Rejoice in the Lord always," doesn't it?

Moishe Rosen
July 1994

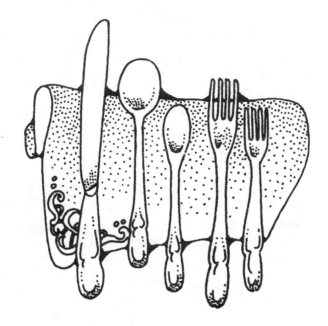

To Moishe Rosen,

who, among other things, has taught me the value of finishing a project.

. . . .

See, Moishe—I did it!

In the Beginning. . .

. . .there were Jews for Jesus who loved to eat but only a few who loved to cook. We were busy with the work God had given us to do, preaching the gospel to our Jewish people. We witnessed for Jesus wherever we could find an opportunity, on the streets of San Francisco, at airports, on college campuses. We testified about Him to anyone who would listen. . .and sometimes to those who didn't want to listen and occasionally to some who were only pretending to listen.

The early days of Jews for Jesus were spent brainstorming, writing, printing and handing out a particular form of gospel tract that we called broadsides. Moishe Rosen, who was blessed with a printing press and a burden to see Jewish people be saved, became the leader (after all, it was his printing press). Our ministry was born, and today we Jews for Jesus still spend a good bit of our time writing, printing and handing out our gospel broadsides on the highways and byways of our land and even in some foreign lands.

In the early days, all our work made us very hungry. Well, some things haven't changed; we still get hungry, and we still love to eat. But whereas at one time only Moishe's wife, Ceil, seemed to know how to cook, now the rest of us have grown up and have our own kitchens, too. During the early '70s, when our work began, the Rosen's were the only ones who lived in one place long enough to call it home. Some of us were fortunate enough to call their home our home, and there we met together to be discipled in the truth of the gospel. We grew together as a family—well, to be honest, we looked more like a tribe. We were a group of ex-hippies and wanderers (my husband, Jhan Moskowitz, claimed he was a pirate) who had been touched by the wonderful grace of God to have our eyes opened to His truth in Y'shua (Jesus).

Today, 20 years later, our family has grown up. There are lots of children running around now, many of us live in our own homes, most of us own microwaves and quite a few of us love to cook. God has blessed us with meaningful work to do for Him. Along with our commitment to bringing Jews to know their Messiah, we also enjoy a good meal now and then. But today, we can cook them ourselves.

So why did we write this cookbook? Because you asked for one! So many want to know what we Jews for Jesus like to eat. One thing will become clear to you immediately: While we love the Jewish dishes of our youth, we also love just about any kind of food. We'll try any recipe that sounds reasonably worth the effort. Though we possess the innate ability to scout out a good Jewish deli no matter where we are (as most Jewish people can), we also love Chinese, Italian, Russian and good old American food. This cookbook reflects the diversity of our backgrounds as well as our tastes.

Just to let you know, we Jews for Jesus do not insist on eating only kosher food although we don't have any problem with those who do. To us, the word kosher means "clean before God." We believe that all Christians have been cleansed before God through the atoning work of the Messiah Y'shua's death. According to rabbinical traditions, the various kosher laws (called kashrut) were created to set the Jewish people apart from the nations. Many of our people believe that by keeping a rigorous set of ordinances, they can be right before God. What encouragement all believers in Y'shua have to know that He offered up the perfect sacrifice when He gave Himself. Thus, we can all rely solely on His provision in Jesus and eat freely according to our conscience.

As I began collecting the recipes for this book, I noticed an international tenor emerging. When the plea went out to the Jews for Jesus staff and extended family for "recipes, send us your recipes," our mailbox began resembling a worldwide postal station. Recipes came from India, Indiana, Argentina and the Bronx. So, you won't find just Jewish recipes in this cookbook, although there are plenty of those that were begged, borrowed and finagled out of our bubbas (grandmothers), tantas (aunts) and mamalas (mamas). But there are also recipes for Mexican, German and Italian dishes. Along with some of the recipes I have included tidbits of information about the contributors.

We hope as you read and enjoy this cookbook that you will feel part of the Jews for Jesus family. God has banded together a mixed bag of believers to serve Him, but we really love Him, and we really love to eat!

In all that you do, eat and drink as unto the Lord, and come, sit down at the banqueting table with us and enjoy our fellowship in Him.

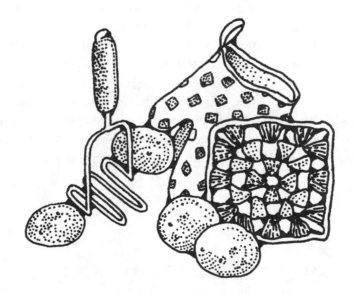

A Mishmash of Dips, Sauces, Salads and Salad Dressings

Mishmash is a Yiddish word for hodgepodge or jumble. It's a good word for this chapter, too, where you'll find recipes that didn't seem to fit in anywhere else. Mishmash also describes the Jews for Jesus family. Our staff and friends hail from all parts of the world. Many of our missionaries are from New York—and their accents give them away. But over the years our ears have also grown accustomed to hearing other accents. We've had West Virginians, Kansas prairie folk, and down-home Oklahomans and Texans on our staff. God has won the hearts of both Iowa farmers and New Mexican housewives to uphold the work of Jews for Jesus, and they're all part of our extended family.

This chapter is as diverse as the people who've contributed to it. Perhaps as you cook and as you eat you'll think about the day when heaven will be filled with representatives from every tribe, tongue and nation. At the Marriage Supper of the Lamb there will be heavenly ambassadors from Brooklyn as well as from Argentina. And until that day, bon appetit.

Zhava Glaser's Spaghetti Sauce

This recipe is one of those measure-and-taste-as-you-go varieties. Zhava, who is from Argentina, insists that some sauces just have to be made this way. This is her mother's recipe, and it is "the best in the world." I tried to get her to write this out in a proper recipe fashion, but decided not to push too hard. Have you ever won an argument with a Jewish mother?

"Fry chopped onions in butter or margarine, together with chopped green peppers and crushed garlic (there are no specific amounts to use - just make sure you use plenty!). When onions are brown and peppers are tender, add 16 ounces of tomato sauce and a (large) pinch of sugar to take out the bite. Add more garlic, be generous with the oregano and throw in three or four bay leaves, cracked in half. Cover and let simmer for one to two hours. Add salt and pepper to taste. This sauce is also good when browned ground beef (seasoned with—you guessed it—garlic and oregano) is added. If sauce gets too thick, add another eight ounces or more of tomato sauce.

The secret to the sauce is to mix it with some cooked pasta and let it sit for a good long time before it's served. Somehow, the American custom of serving sauce and pasta separately does not taste as authentic as when the sauce and pasta are mixed together and allowed to sit - you rob the sauce of its penetrating power."

Easy Shabbat Tomato Sauce

1	(6-ounce) can tomato paste
2	teaspoons chicken bouillon granules
2	teaspoons sugar
2	tomato paste cans water

Bring all ingredients to a boil in medium saucepan; lower heat and simmer for 5 minutes. Serve over noodles or rice. Makes 4 servings.

Iveys's Barbecue Sauce

Joe Ivey is a pilot for Delta Airlines, and the Iveys have been active members of the Fellowship of Christian Airline Personnel. If you're ever flying and see a stewardess or steward wearing a little pin that says F.C.A.P., smile and say, "Praise the Lord!"

3/4	cup catsup
3	teaspoons Worcestershire sauce
2	tablespoons vinegar
1	tablespoon sugar
1 1/2	teaspoons mustard

Bring all ingredients to a boil in a small saucepan; lower heat and simmer for 10 minutes. Makes 1 cup sauce.

Cheryl's Barbecue Sauce

1	(10¾-ounce) can condensed tomato soup
⅓	cup onion, chopped
⅓	cup celery, chopped
1	small clove garlic, minced
1	tablespoon brown sugar
1	tablespoon Worcestershire sauce
1	tablespoon lemon juice or vinegar
1	teaspoon prepared mustard

Mix all ingredients together and pour over browned pieces of boneless round steak or chicken. Simmer on top of stove until meat is tender. Makes enough to cover 1 pound steak or chicken.

Tehina (Sesame Sauce)

This is good served with falafel or as an unusual dressing for a green salad.

3	large cloves garlic, crushed
1	cup hulled sesame seeds, ground fine in blender or food processor
1	cup cold water
½	cup lemon juice
1	teaspoon salt

Mash crushed garlic into a paste (either by hand or in a food processor using the fine blade). Stir in ground sesame seeds. Mix in half of the cold water, lemon juice and salt. Beating well, add up to ½ cup more water, 1 tablespoon at a time, until sauce becomes the consistency of mayonnaise. Taste for seasoning. Makes 1 ½ cups.

Note: This can be made entirely in a food processor.

Horseradish to Knock Your Socks Off

This recipe came from a magazine called *Historic Preservation* (July/August 1979), found in a doctor's waiting room. Myrtle Pancoast, fondly referred to as the "Horseradish Lady of Cross Street" in South Baltimore, Maryland, created this recipe. After you try it your sinuses will be clear for months! We Jews for Jesus call horseradish the "Jewish Dristan." This recipe certainly will do the trick for any stuffy nose.

Soak 2 horseradish roots (2-3 pounds each) in enough water to cover for three to four days to soften. Remove roots to a well-ventilated area. Using a knife (not a potato peeler) scrape the outer bark and discard. Grate the remainder of root. Add 1 tablespoon white vinegar (or 1 tablespoon mayonnaise, if you want a creamy mixture) per cup of grated horseradish. Store in a crock or tightly closed jar in the refrigerator.

John's Dressing

This recipe is from Lori McHugh, a long-time faithful volunteer and worker with Jews for Jesus. She lives in Connecticut with her two children and husband Tom. Says Lori, "Try this recipe if you're tired of the gummy, plastic-like dressings you get in bottles—this can even be your 'house' dressing when friends come to visit.'" But Lori—who's John?

$1^1/_4$	cups orange juice		$^1/_4$	teaspoon pepper
1	cup vegetable oil		1	teaspoon onion, chopped
$1^1/_2$	teaspoons salt		1	clove garlic, crushed
$^1/_2$	teaspoon paprika		1	tablespoon honey

Whirl all ingredients in a blender. Store in tightly covered jar in the refrigerator. Makes about $2^1/_2$ cups of dressing.

Honey Dressing

Use this dressing to spice up a homemade fruit salad.

$^1/_4$	cup honey		1	teaspoon celery seed
$^1/_2$	cup vinegar		1	teaspoon celery salt
$^1/_4$	cup sugar		1	teaspoon onion juice
1	teaspoon dry mustard		1	cup vegetable oil
1	teaspoon paprika			

Mix the honey, vinegar, sugar, mustard and paprika together in a saucepan. Boil three minutes and let cool. Add all other ingredients and beat or shake vigorously in a jar. Keep refrigerated. Makes about 2 cups of dressing.

Hummus

Hummus is a hearty Middle Eastern dip, best served with triangles of heated pita bread. If you can't find pita, crackers or cut-up raw vegetables will do. Hummus can fill in as a light lunch when served with a cucumber-yogurt salad (mix thinly sliced cucumbers with plain yogurt, season to taste with garlic powder, salt and pepper). And speaking of garlic, you can never put too much garlic in hummus. This recipe is a favorite of Tuvya Zaretsky, who is one of the skinniest Jews for Jesus missionaries we know. He can eat as much hummus as he likes.

1	(15-ounce) can chickpeas (also known as garbanzo beans)		1	teaspoon paprika
				dash pepper
2	tablespoons olive oil		2	tablespoons toasted sesame seeds (optional)
2	tablespoons lemon juice		1	teaspoon salt
2	cloves (or more) garlic, minced		1	tablespoon onion, chopped

Drain chickpeas; reserve liquid. In blender, combine chickpeas, one tablespoon liquid, oil, lemon juice, garlic, onion, salt, pepper and paprika. Blend until smooth, pushing down with rubber spatula as necessary. Add more liquid as needed to make a thick, spreadable consistency. Serve with sesame seeds sprinkled over the top if desired. Chill for several hours, but let stand at room temperature for $1/2$ hour before serving. Makes 1 $1/2$ cups.

Sour Cream Dill Dressing

1	cup sour cream	$1/2$	teaspoon garlic salt
$1/2$	cup mayonnaise	$1/8$	teaspoon pepper
1	teaspoon seasoned salt	1	tablespoon dried dill weed

Mix all ingredients well in medium bowl. Cover and refrigerate until serving time. Makes about 1$1/2$ cups dressing.

Bleu Cheese French Dressing

1	small bottle catsup	1	teaspoon grated onion
$1/2$	cup oil	$1 1/2$	tablespoons lemon juice
$1/2$	cup white vinegar	1	teaspoon celery salt
$3/4$	cup sugar	$1/2$	teaspoon paprika
$1/2$	cup crumbled bleu cheese		

Mix all ingredients together in a bowl. Rinse out catsup bottle with $1/2$ cup water and add to rest of ingredients. Beat all together well and store, covered, in refrigerator.

Chart House Bleu Cheese Dressing

$3/4$	cup sour cream
$1/2$	teaspoon dry mustard
$1/3$	teaspoon pepper
$1/4$	teaspoon salt
$1/3$	teaspoon garlic powder
1	teaspoon Worcestershire sauce
$1 1/3$	cups mayonnaise
4	ounces imported Danish bleu cheese, crumbled

In a mixing bowl combine the first 6 ingredients and blend 2 minutes with an electric mixer at low speed. Add mayonnaise and blend 30 seconds at low speed. Increase speed to medium and blend 2 minutes more. Slowly add bleu cheese and blend for 3 minutes more. Refrigerate for 24 hours before serving. Makes about 2 cups.

Garlic Cheese Spread

1   stick margarine ($^1/_2$ cup)
8   ounces cream cheese, softened
2   cloves garlic, finely minced
1   teaspoon dried parsley
1   teaspoon Italian seasoning

Cream all ingredients together well with a wooden spoon. Store in an earthenware crock or covered bowl. Serve with crackers. Makes about $1^1/_2$ cups.

Cheese Spread

1   pound American cheese
2   cups evaporated milk
$1^1/_2$ teaspoons salt
$1^1/_2$ teaspoons dry mustard
2   eggs, beaten

Cut cheese into chunks and melt in double boiler over hot water with milk, salt and mustard. Remove from heat and add beaten eggs. Return to boiler and stir until spread thickens slightly. Remove from heat, cool, stirring often to prevent crust from forming. Store covered in refrigerator. Keeps well. Makes about 4 cups of spread.

Note: You can vary this recipe by adding bacon-flavored bits, Liquid Smoke, chopped green onions, pimento, olives or jalapeno peppers.

Cheese Ball

4   cups cheddar cheese, shredded
6   ounces cream cheese
$^1/_3$ cup mayonnaise
1   teaspoon Worcestershire sauce
$^1/_8$ teaspoon each: onion salt, garlic salt and celery salt
2   teaspoons cooking sherry

Blend all together well.
Add: $^1/_2$ cup chopped, ripe olives

Chill until firm. Shape into one large ball or several small ones.
When firm, roll in: $^1/_3$ cup fresh parsley, minced

Wrap and chill until serving time. These cheese balls make lovely gifts.

Vegetable Dip

1   cup buttermilk
2   cups mayonnaise
4   teaspoons dried parsley flakes
2   teaspoons Italian herb seasoning
1   teaspoon minced garlic
3   teaspoons minced onion
1/2 teaspoon Lawry's seasoned salt
2   teaspoons MSG (Accent)

Mix all ingredients together well.
Let stand at least two hours before serving.
Keeps up to three weeks in refrigerator. Makes 3 cups.

Note: You can thin this dip with milk or buttermilk to make ranch salad dressing.

Taco Dip

2   (8-ounce) packages cream cheese
1   small jar (about 10-ounces) mild taco sauce
1   package (1.5-ounce) dry taco seasoning mix
     tomatoes, sliced (optional)
     green onions, sliced (optional)

Blend all ingredients together well.
Serve with sliced tomatoes and green onions sprinkled over top.
Makes about 2 cups.

Garden Patch Dip

12   ounces cream-style cottage cheese
2   tablespoons each: green pepper, green onion, radishes and carrots, chopped
1/2 teaspoon salt
1/8 teaspoon celery salt
1/8 teaspoon dried dill weed

Combine all ingredients together well and refrigerate until serving time.
Makes 2 cups.
Good served with fresh, raw vegetables.

Spinach Dip

1   (10-ounce) package frozen chopped spinach
1/2   cup green onion, finely chopped
1   cup mayonnaise
1   cup sour cream
1/2   teaspoon garlic powder
      salt and pepper to taste

Cook frozen chopped spinach according to package directions. Squeeze out all water.
Add chopped onion to mayonnaise and sour cream in medium bowl; mix well and season with salt, pepper and garlic powder.
Add drained spinach and mix well.
Chill until serving time.
Makes about 3 cups.

Dill Dip

1   cup sour cream
1   cup mayonnaise
2   tablespoons dill weed

2   tablespoons fresh parsley, chopped
1   tablespoon dehydrated onion flakes
1   tablespoon seasoned salt

Mix all ingredients well in medium bowl.
Cover and refrigerate several hours.
Makes 2 cups.

Boker's Banana-Pineapple-Marshmallow Salad

1   (16-ounce) can pineapple chunks, packed in their own juice
1   cup sugar
4   tablespoons cornstarch
1 1/2   cups miniature marshmallows
2-3   bananas, sliced

Drain pineapple; reserve 1 cup pineapple juice (add water if not enough liquid to make 1 cup).
Add sugar and cornstarch to juice in medium saucepan, bring to a boil; lower heat and simmer until thick.
Set pan in sink or large bowl filled with cold water to cool sauce.
When sauce is cooled, add pineapple, sliced bananas and marshmallows; toss gently.
Chill at least one hour before serving.
Makes 6 servings.

Jo's Refrigerator Pickles

Though not technically a sauce, salad or salad dressing, this recipe ended up in this chapter because we didn't know where else to put it. Our thanks to Jo Koehler in Tennessee for this easy way of pickling cucumbers.

    3¹/₂   pounds cucumbers (about 8 medium)
    2¹/₂   cups sugar
      2   cups cider vinegar
      1   cup water
      1   teaspoon salt
      1   teaspoon celery seed
      1   tablespoon whole mustard seed
    1¹/₂   tablespoons whole mixed pickling spices
      5   pint-size canning jars and lids

Cut cucumbers into ¹/₄" slices. Set aside. In a 5-quart pot combine remaining ingredients and bring to a boil. Add cucumbers and return to a boil. Continue boiling for two minutes more. Spoon cucumber slices, spices and pickling liquid into clean, hot jars. Place lids on and cool. Refrigerate for up to six months. Makes 5 pints.

Minted Brown Rice Salad

2	(13³/₄-ounce) cans chicken broth	¹/₄	teaspoons salt
2	cups raw brown rice	1	cup green onions, sliced
¹/₄	teaspoon salt	1	cup parsley, chopped
¹/₃	cup lemon juice	2	tablespoons dried
¹/₄	cup olive oil		mint leaves

In a medium saucepan, bring broth to a boil over moderately high heat; add rice and ¹/₄ teaspoon salt. Reduce heat to low, cover pan and cook 40-45 minutes, until liquid is absorbed and rice is tender. Remove pan from heat, add lemon juice, olive oil, and toss to mix. Allow rice to sit 30 minutes; mix in green onions, parsley and dried mint. Makes 8 servings.

Watergate Salad

Although the recipe for this salad bears a somewhat unreliable name, the salad is anything but. Anna Maria Hasch, whose name appears often in this cookbook, submitted this recipe.

    1   (20-ounce) can crushed pineapple
    1   box instant pistachio pudding mix
    5   ounces miniature marshmallows
    9   ounces frozen non-dairy whipped topping
  ¹/₂   cup almonds or walnuts, chopped

Do not drain pineapple; empty into a large bowl, add pudding mix and stir until well incorporated. Add marshmallows; fold in whipped topping. Sprinkle with chopped nuts and refrigerate until serving time. Makes 4-6 servings.

Marinated Garden Salad

1	large stalk broccoli, cut into bite-sized pieces
1	head cauliflower, separated into small flowerets
$1/2$	pound carrots, sliced $1/4$" thick
$1/3$	cup red wine vinegar
$1/4$	cup oil
2	teaspoons dried dill weed
$1/2$	teaspoon salt
$1/8$	teaspoon pepper
1	clove garlic, minced
2	cups cherry tomatoes, halved
1	small zucchini, sliced paper-thin
1	(8-ounce) can sliced, black or green olives

Place broccoli, cauliflower and carrots in a large saucepan, add 1-2" water and cook over medium heat until crispy-done. Let cool. Drain and reserve cooking liquid. Combine liquid and spices and pour over all vegetables in serving dish, cover and marinate in refrigerator at least 2 hours before serving. Makes 6 servings.

Carolyn Balswick's Salad #1

Each summer Jews for Jesus holds intensive witnessing campaigns on the streets of New York City. Hundreds of thousands of gospel broadsides are handed out, one-by-one, by volunteer Jewish believers and staff members. It is a thrilling, energizing and tiring adventure. Moishe Rosen's attitude about the campaigners, who are mainly young, energetic students and volunteers, is "work them hard, feed them well." One of the best cooks the campaigners have ever been fed by is Carolyn Balswick. She is full of energy herself and known around Jews for Jesus for her many, colorful pairs of eyeglasses.

Dressing:

$1/2$	cup oil
2	tablespoons red wine vinegar
2	tablespoons lemon juice
1	teaspoon sugar
$1/2$	teaspoon dry mustard
$1/2$	teaspoon salt

Salad:

	red grapes
2	oranges, sectioned
2	avocados, sliced
$1/4$	red onion, sliced thin
	mixed greens

Shake all dressing ingredients in jar. Pour over fruit/vegetable mixture in large bowl. Refrigerate until serving time. Makes 4-6 servings.

Carolyn Balswick's Salad #2

3 large tomatoes, coarsely chopped
2 cucumbers, coarsely chopped
2 green peppers, coarsely chopped
1 small red onion, chopped fine
1 cup black olives, sliced in half
1/2 pound feta cheese, cubed
1/2 cup bottled Italian dressing (or more to taste)

Toss all ingredients together with Italian dressing. Chill until serving time. Makes 6 servings.

Corn Vinaigrette

When guests are initially served this dish, they may ask, "What, cold corn?" But whenever this dish appears on a potluck or picnic table, it's one of the first salads to disappear.

Salad:
1 20-ounce package frozen corn, cooked, drained and cooled
1/2 cup green pepper, diced
1/2 cup green onion, sliced thin
1 cup cherry tomatoes, halved

Vinaigrette dressing:
1/2 cup oil
1/4 cup cider vinegar
1 1/2 teaspoons lemon juice
3 tablespoons parsley, chopped
1 1/2-2 teaspoons salt
1 teaspoon sugar
1/2 teaspoon dried basil
1/4 teaspoon cayenne pepper

Mix all ingredients for vinaigrette in a bowl; pour over assembled vegetables in serving dish and toss together well. Chill until serving time. Makes 6 servings.

Potato Salad in a Minute

Submitted by Gina Moss, this salad is especially valuable if you have a baby or small children at home as it can be made in a hurry.

Figure one medium potato per person. Microwave (in loosely covered bowl) or boil in skin until a fork pierces the center of the potatoes easily. Run potatoes under cold water until cool enough to handle. Peel while under the water; the skins should come off easily. Cut in to bite-sized chunks and cool in the refrigerator (you can play with the baby in the meantime). When ready to serve, toss potatoes with your favorite bottled salad dressing, such as Caesar, ranch or Italian. If you're counting calories, use a low-calorie or nonfat variety.

Suggestion: Keep a few cooked potatoes in the refrigerator for whenever you're in the mood for potato salad.

Potato Salad in a Few More Minutes

Submitted by Lois Link, this salad takes just a few more minutes to make than the previous recipe.

5	medium potatoes, peeled and cooked
1	teaspoon salt
	dash white pepper
2	tablespoons green onion, chopped
2	tablespoons pimento, chopped
3	hard-boiled eggs, chopped
1/4	cup celery, diced
1 1/4	cup mayonnaise (can be low-calorie variety)

Cut cooked potatoes into bite-sized pieces. Add remaining ingredients; toss to mix lightly. Refrigerate until serving time. Makes 6-8 servings.

Waterloo Potato Salad

Family reunions at Sue Rothberg's parents' home in Waterloo, Indiana are "warm, noisy and fun." A super abundance of food was the main strategy for a memorable time together. This recipe for potato salad hails from Sue's grandmother, Grandma Mortoff, and Sue says it's won all sorts of family "competitions."

4-5	medium potatoes, peeled
3	hard-boiled eggs
	small onion, diced
3-4	stalks celery, diced
3/4	cup mayonnaise
1/4	cup sour cream
2	teaspoons vinegar
2	teaspoons sugar
1/2	teaspoon mustard (optional)
	salt and pepper

Boil potatoes in salted water to cover until done. Cool. Dice potatoes and eggs. Mix gently with remaining ingredients. Chill several hours or overnight before serving. Makes 6 servings.

Summer Rice Salad

3	cups cooked, cold rice
1/3	cup olive oil
1	tablespoon salt
1	teaspoon pepper
1	teaspoon dried dillweed
2	(6-7 ounce) cans tuna fish, drained
1	cup diced celery
1/4	cup red wine vinegar
1/4	cup sliced, black olives

In a large bowl combine rice and olive oil.
Mix well, coating each grain.
Sprinkle on salt, pepper and dillweed.
Mix well.
Add tuna, celery and olives.
Pour in vinegar and toss.
For finishing touches sprinkle some dill on the top.
Chill before serving.
Serves 4 as a main dish or 6-8 as a side dish with soup or sandwiches.

Warm Cabbage Salad with Goat Cheese

In this recipe, the goat cheese melts into the warm salad and counters the vinegar by giving the salad a unique blend of pungent flavors. Thanks to Mitch Forman, our resident chef-turned-missionary.

2	ounces walnut oil
2	ounces olive oil
1	clove garlic, chopped
1	tablespoon fresh ginger, chopped
1	small head red cabbage, shredded
4	ounces balsamic vinegar
4	ounces walnuts, toasted and chopped
4	ounces goat cheese, cut into small pieces

Heat the oil in a large pot.
Add the garlic and ginger and saute for 15 seconds.
Add the cabbage and balsamic vinegar, and cook until the cabbage is soft but still a bit firm (about 10 minutes).
Divide the cabbage onto four plates.
Sprinkle the walnuts and goat cheese over the top.
Makes 4 servings.

Spring Salad

2	avocados, sliced
2	pink grapefruits, sectioned
1	pint strawberries, hulled
4	small heads Bibb lettuce, washed, dried and torn up
$3/4$	cup sugar
$1/3$	cup vinegar
1	teaspoon dry mustard
1	teaspoon salt
$1^1/_2$	tablespoons onion, grated
1	cup vegetable oil
$1^1/_2$	tablespoons poppy seeds

Arrange the first four ingredients evenly (and artfully) on eight salad plates. Blend remaining ingredients together in a blender or shaker; serve over salad. Makes 8 servings.

Jo Ann Farris's Dinner When There's Nothing in the House

(Serve with Dan's Famous Salad)

Remove bagels from fridge (frozen variety is fine).
Cut bagels in half.
Remove cheese from fridge (any variety is fine).
Slice cheese.
Place cheese on top of bagel (put on a lot).
Place in toaster oven.
Bake for 5-6 minutes at 400°.
Top bagels with a lot of vegetarian bacon bits.
Place in toaster oven or conventional oven for a few more minutes until cheese melts.

Says Jo Ann: "In 1984, when I was teaching skating until very late at night, we had very little time for shopping.
We began to make it a practice to always keep our fridge stocked with bagels.
This dinner became a favorite in our house.
Eventually, as the years passed, my husband Dan got sick of cheese on bagels, but for me, they are still a favorite."

Dan's Famous Salad

Chop or tear off some lettuce and put it in a bowl.
Sprinkle on some Parmesan cheese.
Sprinkle on some Schilling salad toppings.
Top with croutons (a whole lot).
Serve with low-cal dressing.

Chopped Herring Salad

1 (12-ounce) jar herring fillets in wine sauce
1 large apple, peeled and quartered
1 small onion, sliced
1 slice rye bread
1 hard-boiled egg
1 teaspoon vegetable oil
1/2 teaspoon sugar

Drain herring, reserving liquid.
In a bowl, soak rye bread in reserved liquid. In the bowl of a food processor place herring, apple, onion, soaked bread with any remaining liquid and egg; process until chopped fine but not mashed.
Stir in oil and sugar.
Makes 6-8 appetizer servings.

Grandma Weininger's Appetizers

3/4 cup mayonnaise
1/2 cup Parmesan cheese
1/3 cup green onion, chopped
dash Worcestershire sauce
salt and pepper
sourdough English muffins

Combine first five ingredients together well and spread on English muffins.
Place under broiler until cheese melts, or bake at 350° (can be baked in toaster oven) for 5 minutes.
Makes 2-4 servings.

Soup:
A Little Bit of This, a Little Bit of That

Many people believe that a good bowl of chicken soup is a cure-all for a cold, the flu, a fever or whatever else ails you. It's good comfort food. Our mothers believed in this bit of wisdom, as did their mothers before them and their mothers before that. Perhaps even Sarah served Abraham some nice chicken soup from time to time. In more recent years, medical studies have shown that chicken soup, while not containing any magic medicinal substances, does work wonders in treating the common cold. Our mothers could have told those doctors and scientists that!

Another soup that has descended through many generations of grandmothers and great-grandmothers is a hearty mushroom barley soup, often made with imported dried mushrooms. Such mushrooms are available in most supermarkets these days. In this chapter, you'll find a mushroom barley soup recipe that came from someone's mother, although we're not sure whose.

There's an old folktale about "stone soup," in which some peasants are fooled by two hungry transients into believing they can make a delicious soup out of rocks. Into the bottom of a large pot went a small stone. Then the peasants are tricked into contributing other things—potatoes, meat and vegetables—to make this magic soup. In the end they marvel at how such a delicious soup was made from a stone. The moral of the story is that your appetite can often lead you astray and allow you to be fooled by simpletons. Our Jewish grandfathers led us to believe that this was an old Jewish folktale, but our Italian, French and Spanish friends remember this story from their youths, too. One thing is for certain in this cookbook: All the recipes are 100% stone-free, and delicious!

Mushroom Barley Soup

3-4	pounds beef flanken or short ribs	1½	cups onion, diced
14	cups water	½	cup medium pearl barley
1	large onion, peeled	½	cup fresh parsley, chopped
1	stalk celery	2	teaspoons dried dillweed
1	tablespoon salt	1	cup milk
1	ounce dried mushrooms, rinsed, drained and cut in small pieces	¼	cup flour
		3	carrots, sliced ¼" thick

Rinse meat and put in a large pot. Add water and bring to a boil over high heat.
Skim off foam and add onion, celery and salt. Return to a boil.
Lower heat; simmer, covered for 1 hour. Add dried mushrooms and simmer 30 minutes.
Remove and discard onion and celery.
Add diced onion, carrots, barley, parsley and dillweed. Simmer for 30 minutes.
Remove meat to a plate.
Mix milk with flour and stir into soup.
Bring to a boil, reduce heat to moderately low and simmer 10 minutes, stirring occasionally.
Remove meat from bones and cut into bite-sized pieces; discard fat and bones.
Return meat to soup and cook 5 minutes more. Add salt and pepper to taste.
Makes 8 servings.

Cabbage Borscht

1½	pounds beef brisket or chuck roast
1	bunch beets, peeled and sliced (use beet tops another time)
1	large onion, chopped
1	medium head cabbage
1	(28-ounce) can tomato puree
½	teaspoon pepper
3	tablespoons sugar
1	tablespoon salt
	juice of 1 lemon (3 tablespoons)

Place meat over high heat in a 5-quart pot; sear until well-browned on all sides.
Add beets and onions; lower heat and cook until beets are tender, about 15 minutes.
Remove beets, shred them and put them back into the pot with the cabbage,
tomato puree, and enough water to cover.
Add salt, pepper, sugar and lemon juice.
Bring to a boil, skimming off foam as it rises to the top.
Lower heat, cover and simmer 2 hours.
Makes 8 servings.

Cheese and Corn Chowder

$1/2$	cup water		2	cups creamed corn
2	cups diced raw potatoes		$1^1/2$	cups milk
1	cup sliced carrots		$2/3$	cup cheddar cheese, grated
1	cup chopped celery			
1	teaspoon salt			
$1/4$	teaspoon pepper			

Combine first six ingredients in a saucepan; cover and bring to a boil.
Simmer over low heat for 10 minutes.
Add creamed corn and simmer 5 minutes more.
Add milk and grated cheese; stir until cheese melts and chowder is heated through.
Do not boil.
Makes 4-6 servings.

Delores Howard's Hungarian Potato Soup

Delores Howard graces the Chicago branch of Jews for Jesus with her faithful presence and prayer support.
Besides being a long-standing volunteer and friend, she is also a terrific cook!

4	tablespoons butter or margarine
2	large stalks celery, diced small
1	medium onion, diced
2	heaping tablespoons flour
5	cups water
4	medium potatoes, peeled and diced
	salt and pepper
4	ounces wide noodles, uncooked and broken into squares
	paprika
3	heaping tablespoons sour cream

In a large saucepan, sauté celery and onion in melted butter or margarine.
After vegetables have softened and are beginning to turn yellow, mix in flour and stir well.
Add water, potatoes, and salt and pepper to taste.
Raise the heat to almost boiling, then lower heat and cook, covered, for 1 hour.
Stir occasionally. In separate pan, cook noodles in boiling water until nearly done.
Drain and add to soup.
Sprinkle soup generously with paprika and turn off heat.
Add sour cream, stir and serve.
Makes 6 servings.

Spicy Fish Chowder

From that great cook and Jews for Jesus booster in Connecticut, Lori McHugh, comes this fish chowder. It tastes so good your guests will think you caught the fish, skinned and boned them, and then slaved all day over a hot stove to make this chowder.

1   cup chopped green pepper
$^1/_3$ cup chopped onion
1   large clove garlic, minced
1   bay leaf
1   teaspoon dried basil
$^1/_2$ teaspoon dried oregano
2   tablespoons olive oil
$^1/_2$ cup dry red wine
1   ($10^1/_2$-ounce) can condensed tomato soup
1   soup can water
$^1/_4$ cup fresh parsley, chopped
1   pound fish filets, any kind, cut in 2" pieces
1   ($10^1/_2$-ounce) can condensed chicken broth

In a large saucepan cook green pepper, onion and garlic with seasonings in olive oil until tender. Add wine and simmer 2 minutes. Add all other ingredients. Cover and simmer 10 minutes, stirring gently now and then. Remove bay leaf. Add fresh ground pepper to taste. Makes 6 servings.

A Chicken Soup Story

Jo Ann Farris is an expert ice skater. When she first met her husband Dan she was living with her Grandma Fannie. Grandma made chicken soup every week, and Jo Ann invited him over for some. Jo Ann had neglected to tell Dan that sometimes her grandmother forgot to take the chicken necks out of the soup, which was exactly what happened the evening Dan came for dinner. Since this was the beginning of their relationship, impressions were very important. But what do you do with a man who quietly remarks, "You know, I have a mouth full of vertebrae, what am I supposed to do?" Dan quickly went to spit out the bones before Grandma knew what was happening, and soon after, Jo Ann married him.

Chicken Soup from a Jewish Mother

Some of us were fortunate enough, and attentive enough, to learn from our mothers while they were busy in the kitchen. The rest of us have learned to cook by trial and error (sometimes many errors). This recipe for chicken soup is fairly easy—it takes little more than throwing a chicken in a pot and covering it with water. Although not necessary, a kosher chicken may taste better than a regular chicken for making soup. If you're fortunate enough to live near a kosher butcher, then by all means try a kosher chicken for this soup.

5	pounds chicken parts (backs, necks, etc.)	1¼	tablespoons salt
3¼	quarts water	3	carrots, peeled and sliced
2	onions, peeled and halved		several sprigs parsley
2	cloves garlic, peeled and halved	1	teaspoon dried dillweed

Place first four ingredients in a large pot (at least 5 quarts). Bring to a boil, skimming off fat as it rises to top. Lower heat, cover pot and simmer for 2 hours. Add carrots, salt and parsley; simmer 1 hour more. Stir in dillweed; heat for 15 minutes and serve. Makes 12 cups of soup.

Note: *This is even better if refrigerated overnight before serving. The hardened fat can be removed before re-heating. This soup can also be strained into a clean pot and served with sliced carrots and small bits of the chicken.*

Cream of Cauliflower Soup

This recipe comes to us from Sue McHugh in Hamburg, New York, via the Liberated Wailing Wall members, to whom she serves this soup whenever they travel through her town.

1	(10-ounce) package frozen cauliflower
2	cups chicken broth
2	cups milk
2	slices white bread, crumbled
4	ounces sharp cheddar cheese, shredded or grated

Steam cauliflower in broth in a saucepan. Whirl in blender and remove. Blend milk, cheese and bread. Combine both mixtures in saucepan and heat together. Makes 6 servings.

NOTE: *Can also be made using 10 ounces of frozen broccoli.*

Anna's Soup Kitchen

Anna Marie Hasch could open her own soup kitchen. While not busy attending Jews for Jesus functions in Skokie and tending to her husband, Norm, and their children, Mrs. Hasch has gained a reputation as a fine cook. She says that one of her tricks for a good soup is to use distilled water. All of her soups included here make at least 6 servings.

Anna's French Canadian Pea Soup

In a large pot, add 4 cups water, ½ pound dried green split peas, ½ cup chopped onion, ½ cup chopped celery, ½ cup sliced carrots, ½ to 1 cup cubed potatoes, 1 or 2 beef or chicken bouillon cubes, and salt to taste. Bring to a boil; simmer until vegetables are done.

Fry 2 slices of turkey bacon, drain and crumble. Add bacon to the soup. Add ¼ cup light cream and 1 tablespoon butter. Heat and serve.

Anna's Dutch Pea Soup

In a large pot, combine 1½ cups dried green split peas; 3 quarts of water, 2 or 3 leeks, thinly sliced (white part only); 2 medium onions, chopped; 1 stalk celery, chopped (include leafy top); 2-4 medium potatoes, cubed; ½ pound diced turkey ham. Bring soup to a boil, lower heat and simmer until vegetables are done. Season with salt and a little soy sauce.

Anna's Onion Soup

In a large pot, combine 3 quarts of water; 2 carrots, sliced; 2 stalks of celery, chopped; 2 medium onions, halved; salt; pepper; a handful of dried onion skins; a few green or red pepper strips; 2 fresh or a small can of tomatoes; a little parsley; 2-3 pounds of either beef shanks, short ribs or beef neck bones and 3-4 beef bouillon cubes or 1 package dried onion soup mix. Simmer together until meat and vegetables are tender. Strain into a clean pot. Refrigerate broth to be used for onion soup.

To make onion soup: Slice 4 pounds of onions. Sauté in 3-6 tablespoons butter or margarine until tender and slightly browned. Add strained soup stock (above). Simmer together a few minutes.

To serve: Place a piece of toasted French or Italian bread in a heatproof bowl and cover it with grated Swiss or Mozzarella cheese. Ladle in soup. Place bowls under broiler for a few minutes until cheese is melted.

Anna's French Lima Bean Soup

Sort and wash 1 pound of dried lima beans. Add to 8 cups of water, bring to a boil, reduce heat and simmer 2 minutes. Cover, turn off heat and let stand one hour. Then cook for 1 ½ hours over medium low flame; add a little oil to the cooking water to keep beans from foaming over.

In a skillet combine ½ pound bulk turkey sausage chunks, ½ cup chopped onion, 1 cup cubed ham; cook until meat is done, drain off fat and add to soup. Add 1 can condensed golden mushroom soup, 2 to 3 tablespoons of catsup, ¼ teaspoon garlic powder, 1 bay leaf; cover and simmer 20 minutes. Add cooked lima beans and heat.

Mother-in-Law's Vegetable Barley Soup

One of the greatest challenges in getting a recipe from a Jewish mother is that she often carries her recipes around in her head, but they're never written down on paper. This particular recipe was carefully copied down while the soup was being made. It was a funny process, with constant interruptions of "how many handfuls of parsley do you think that was?" and "but how do you know how much salt it needs?" In the end, the women remained friends although they probably will never attempt to cook together again.

3	quarts water
1¹/₂	teaspoons salt
2	chicken legs
2	chicken thighs
¹/₂-³/₄	pound fresh string beans, cut in 1¹/₂" pieces
4	small zucchini, peeled and cubed
¹/₂	of a small kohlrabi, peeled and cubed
2	parsnips, peeled and cubed
3	carrots, peeled and cubed
2	stalks celery, sliced thin
²/₃	cup pearl barley, washed
1	onion, cut in quarters
1	cup parsley, finely chopped
1	cup parsnips tops, finely chopped

Bring water and salt to a boil in a 5-quart pot. Add remaining ingredients and bring to a boil again; lower heat, loosely cover pot and simmer over low flame for 2 hours. Remove chicken; let cool and remove from bones; return meat to soup. Makes at least 16 cups soup.

Note: *This tastes better the second day.*

French Onion Soup

This recipe comes from a Jews for Jesus supporter who lives in France.

3	tablespoons butter
1	tablespoon vegetable oil
4	medium yellow onions, peeled and thinly sliced
1	teaspoon salt
1	bay leaf
¹/₂	teaspoon sugar
2	tablespoons flour
2	quarts of beef broth, heated
	Parmesan cheese, grated
	a few thin slices of Swiss or Gruyere cheese

In a 5-quart pot, melt butter over medium heat; add vegetable oil, onions and salt.
Stir.
Cook over low heat 30 minutes, stirring occasionally. Add sugar and flour.
Cook 2 minutes until brown.
Add heated broth and bay leaf. Simmer 30 minutes.
Pour into ovenproof bowls, top each with 2 tablespoons Parmesan cheese and a slice of Swiss cheese.
Bake in 325° oven for 15 minutes, or until cheese melts.
Makes 8-10 servings.

Turkey Wild Rice Soup

Anyone with the unlikely name of Lois Link probably has to be a little different. And anyone who worked with Jews for Jesus for as long and in as many different roles as Lois Link also has to be a little crazy (although nicely so!). Lois shared an apartment with Gina Moss while she was still Gina Ciavolino (a nice Jewish girl with an Italian name). Whenever Gina knew that Lois was going to make this soup, she canceled whatever plans she'd made for the evening. Gina was even once heard to make this funny, but morbid, statement: "Lois, when I die, I want my coffin filled with this soup!" Gina Moss is alive and well and living in Cincinnati; Lois is alive and well and still cooking!

1	quart condensed chicken broth
2	cups water
1/2	cup rinsed wild rice, raw
1/2	cup green onions, chopped
1	cup celery, chopped
1/2	cup margarine, melted
3/4	cup flour
1/2	teaspoon salt
1/4	teaspoon poultry seasoning
	dash of white pepper
2	cups half and half
1 1/2	cups cubed turkey or chicken, cooked
8	slices turkey bacon, cooked crisp and crumbled
1	tablespoon chopped pimiento
1/2	pound fresh mushrooms, sliced (optional)

Combine the first five ingredients in a large soup pot, bring to a boil, reduce heat, cover and simmer 40 minutes or until rice is tender.

In a medium saucepan, add spices to melted margarine; add flour and cook, stirring constantly for 1 minute. Put these ingredients into a blender and process at low speed, gradually adding half and half. Return mixture to saucepan and heat over low heat, stirring constantly until thickened slightly.

Add this mixture gradually to broth in large soup pot, stirring constantly to avoid lumps.

Add chopped turkey or chicken, bacon, pimiento and mushrooms (optional).

Makes 8 servings.

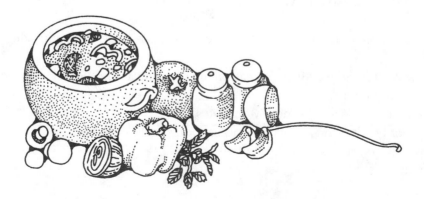

Fifteen Ways to Bake a Brisket, or What to Make Instead of Chicken

Eager to be a good wife, a young newlywed asked her mother-in-law for recipes for her husband's favorite foods. She followed the instructions to the letter and soon became a good cook. But after several years of cooking a certain roast exactly as specified, the young woman was still puzzled by the recipe. One day she mustered up enough courage to question the unusual procedure.

"Mother," she asked, "why do I need to cut off both ends of the meat when I make Sam's favorite pot roast?"

The mother-in-law responded simply, "Well, that's how my mother always made it for Papa. My older sister Sarah makes it that way, too. Why don't you ask her?"

The next time the young wife saw her husband's Aunt Sarah, she inquired about the pot roast recipe. "I don't know," Aunt Sarah shrugged. "I just make it the way Mama taught me. I never thought to ask why. It's always worked for her, so why should I change it?"

Still puzzled, the young woman determined that she would find the answer. One day she drove 150 miles to the rest home where her husband's eighty year-old grandmother lived. After affectionate greetings and small talk, she blurted out, "Grandma, I must ask you this question. Why do we always cut the ends off the meat when we make your recipe for pot roast?"

The old lady looked surprised for a moment; then, a smile creased her wrinkled face, and her eyes twinkled behind the trifocals perched at the end of her nose as she explained. "I would always cut the ends off and use them another time because the butcher used to cut the meat too big to fit my roasting pan."

You're smiling; so are we. Ceil Rosen told us this story, and we thought it was a fitting beginning to this chapter. Before you run out to make Mama Cohen's Company Roast make sure you have a big enough pan!

Mama Cohen's Company Roast

Mama Cohen was a Jewish believer of Hungarian descent, and she cooked as beautifully as she praised the Lord. This dish is ideal for company because it can be assembled well in advance of serving time and requires no last-minute carving.

- 3 pounds beef brisket or other lean roast
- 2 large onions, sliced
- 1 tablespoon oil (optional)
- 2 (6-ounce) cans mushroom steak sauce
  salt, pepper and garlic powder to taste

Do not cut off the ends! Place roast, fat side up, on a rack in a shallow pan and cook for 1 hour at 350°. Remove roast and let cool enough for easy handling. Cut meat into thin, even slices and set aside. Sauté onion slices in oil if desired (they can be used raw, but the flavor is nicer if they are cooked just until transparent). Assemble all the ingredients in oven-to-table casserole or glass baking dish as follows: Layer the meat slices in the bottom of a baking pan; season to taste with salt, pepper and garlic powder; spread the mushroom sauce evenly over the meat, then arrange the sliced onions on top of the sauce. Cover the pan with a lid or aluminum foil and bake for 1 hour at 350° until meat is well done and flavors are blended. Makes 8-10 servings.

On Genealogies and Brisket

Have you ever thought about investigating your family tree? The Saltzmans, a delightful couple in Minneapolis, have been unearthing their family's genealogy for years. Mr. Saltzman has carefully written down, in a beautiful calligraphic hand, the information he and his wife have discovered. It's all contained on several scrolls of heavy white paper and is truly a treasure for their family. Records, birth certificates and photographs have aided the Saltzmans in their search, and they've had a wonderful, meaningful time finding out about their ancestors.

So what does a family tree have to do with recipes (after all, this is a cookbook)? It seems that the Saltzmans are great cooks as well as historians. They've submitted this unusual recipe for brisket that's barbecued in a teriyaki-based sauce. And who knows? Maybe their recipe will inspire you to begin unearthing your family tree as well.

- 7 pounds beef brisket
  catsup
- 1 (10-ounce) bottle teriyaki sauce
- 1 envelope dry onion soup mix
- 2 tablespoons brown sugar

Place brisket in a baking pan. Cover with catsup and pour entire bottle of teriyaki sauce over it. Pour onion soup mix on top of meat and sprinkle it with brown sugar. Cover and bake at 350° for 2 ½ hours (for a smaller brisket, perhaps 2 pounds, cook for 1 hour or so). Serves many - at least 12.

Authentic Chicken Fried Steak (From One Who Knows)

Alan Bond, son-in-law of Moishe and Ceil Rosen, grew up in a nice, Gentile home in Shawnee, Oklahoma. While his wife Lyn grew up on blintzes and potato kugel, Alan ate chicken fried steak, grits and gravy. After they were married, Lyn, eager to please her Oklahoma husband, learned to make his favorite chicken fried steak. Her recipe is included here and is dedicated to all those born with (or without) a Midwest twang.

	oil or shortening
1	pound cube steak, in 4 pieces or 1 pound round steak, pounded thin with a meat mallet, tenderized with meat tenderizer, cut in 4 pieces
1	egg
1/2	cup flour
1/2	cup yellow corn meal
	salt and pepper to taste
1/4	teaspoon paprika

Heat a heavy skillet containing enough oil or shortening to cover the bottom to 1/4".

On a large plate scramble an egg.
On a piece of waxed paper (or a second plate) combine flour, corn meal and spices.

Rinse meat and towel dry.
Dip each piece in egg, then in flour mixture.
Fry in hot oil 3-5 minutes on each side, depending on the thickness of the meat.
Serve with gravy: Remove the meat from the skillet, and keep it warm in low oven.
To drippings in pan add leftover flour mixture.
Remove from heat, stirring constantly until thickened.
Makes 4 servings.

Creamed Hamburger and Cabbage

3/4	pound ground beef	1/4	teaspoon salt
1	tablespoon instant minced onion	1	teaspoon steak sauce
4	cups cabbage, chopped	1	(10 1/2-ounce) can condensed cream of
1/2	teaspoon celery seed		celery soup
1/2	teaspoon paprika	1/4	cup milk

Cook beef, breaking up with a fork, in skillet until meat loses its red color.
Add onion and cabbage and cook until lightly browned.
Add remaining ingredients; cover and simmer about 10 minutes.
Makes 4 servings.

Mom's Meatballs

The credit for this unusual recipe goes to the mother of Evan Pepper, a Jewish believer who lives in Los Angeles. The combination of grape jelly and bottle chili sauce may sound strange at first, but it produces a genuine sweet-and-sour flavor. Jewish people seem to have a penchant for sweet-and-sour foods. Perhaps it comes from living with the hope of redemption in the midst of trial. Perhaps!

6	ounces grape jelly
1	cup water
2	tablespoons lemon juice
1	(12-ounce) bottle chili sauce
2	pounds lean ground beef
2	eggs
1/2	cup cornflakes, crumbled a bit
1	teaspoon salt

Sauce: Mix jelly, water, lemon juice and chili sauce in a saucepan; bring to a boil.

Meatballs: Mix beef, eggs, cornflakes and salt; shape into small balls (the size of a walnut) and add gently to the sauce.
Simmer together 25-35 minutes.
Makes 6-8 servings.

Note: It is best to make these one day, refrigerate, skim off hardened fat and re-heat to be served the next day.

Enchiladas from One Who Didn't Know

Janie-Sue Wertheim was raised in Connecticut but like all good Jews for Jesus, ended up living someplace else once she joined our staff. She claims that before she moved to the West Coast, she "had never even seen a tortilla," let alone cooked one. Her recipe for enchiladas definitely does not let on to the fact that she came face-to-face with tortillas only a few years ago.

Sauce:

1	(28-ounce) can tomato sauce
1	(8-ounce) can stewed tomatoes
1	teaspoon chili powder (or more to taste)
1/2	teaspoon ground cumin (or more to taste)
1	teaspoon dried oregano
1/2	teaspoon salt
1	onion, chopped

Combine all ingredients in a saucepan, mashing up tomatoes. Simmer gently for 10-15 minutes.

Filling:
- 1   pound lean ground beef
- 1   green pepper, seeded and diced
- 1   onion, chopped
- 2   cups cooked brown rice
- 1   teaspoon chili powder
- 1/2   teaspoon each salt and ground cumin
- 2   cups cheddar cheese, grated

Brown beef in a skillet and drain off fat. Add green pepper and onion. Cook until tender. Add remaining ingredients, except for rice and cheese. Cook two minutes more until taste is well blended. Add the rice, mixing gently; add about 1/3 cup sauce.

Warm 12 burrito-size flour tortillas in an oven for a minute or so. Fill the tortillas with the meat-and-rice mixture, fold over gently and place in a greased baking pan. Pour the remaining sauce over all and sprinkle 2 cups of grated cheddar cheese over top. Bake 350° for 45 minutes or until hot and bubbly. Makes 6-8 servings for those with hearty appetites.

Tzimmes Shabbat Nachum

Joel Kleinbaum is a man of many wonders. He's a musician, a missionary, a historian and a well-known cook among the Jews for Jesus. And, at the time of this writing, he's still single!

Tzimmes is a traditional Jewish dish of sweet and white potatoes, carrots and dried fruits. Shabbat Nachum was a particular Friday night worship service at the congregation that Jews for Jesus had formed in Los Angeles. That night the Old Testament passage of Isaiah 40 was read in Hebrew, "Nachum, nachum, ami." This translates, "Comfort ye, comfort ye my people." If this sounds complicated, don't worry. You can make this dish without understanding a word of Hebrew. Thank God you don't have to be a Hebrew scholar to recognize good food. Tzimmes Shabbat Nachum can be prepared any day of the week.

- 1   large onion, coarsely chopped
- 1   tablespoon vegetable oil
- 1 1/4   pounds lean chuck or brisket, cut in bite-size pieces
- 1/2   cup water
- 1/3   cup honey
-     salt, pepper
- 1/2   teaspoon cinnamon
- 1/2   teaspoon ground allspice
- 2   medium or one large sweet potato, quartered
- 2   potatoes, quartered
- 6   good-sized carrots, sliced in rounds
- 2   large apples

Sauté the onion in some oil for several minutes, add the meat and brown, adding salt and pepper to taste. Add water, honey, cinnamon and allspice. Bring to a boil and add carrots and both types of potatoes. Return to a boil, then simmer, covered. While simmering, peel and cut the apples into small cubes; add to the pot. Cook over very low flame or in 250° oven for 3 hours. Makes 4-6 servings.

Bachelor's Hamburger Stew

Another of Joel's recipes—so called because it only uses one pot.

>   oil for sauté
> 1   onion, chopped
> 1   pound ground beef
> 1   (15-ounce) can stewed tomatoes
> 1/2 cup beef bouillon or tomato juice (optional)
> 1/3 cup pearl barley
>   salt, pepper, thyme to taste
>   one or two crushed garlic cloves
> 4   carrots, sliced
> 1   large or 2 small potatoes, diced bite-sized
> 1   (10-ounce) package frozen corn
>   any other fresh or cooked vegetables you might have leftover

Sauté the onion in some oil until soft and translucent.
Add meat and brown.
Pour off grease.
Add tomatoes and their liquid, plus 1/2 cup water, beef bouillon or tomato juice.
Bring to a boil and add barley and seasonings.
Cover and simmer over low flame.
Add the vegetables in order of the length of time it takes for them to cook.
The stew is done when all the vegetables and the barley are cooked (45-60 minutes).
Makes 4 servings.

One-Pot Italian Beef Stew

This recipe comes from Gina Ciavolino Moss, a nice Jewish girl with an Italian father and a Jewish husband.

> 2   tablespoons olive oil
> 2   pounds beef stew meat, cut in bite-sized cubes
> 3   (14 1/2-ounce) cans Italian-style stewed tomatoes
> 1   package instant onion soup mix (dry)
> 1   (16-ounce) package frozen sliced zucchini
> 1/2 pound small mushrooms (or larger ones, sliced)
> 1/2 teaspoon garlic powder

In a large Dutch oven, heat olive oil and brown meat slowly. Add 2 cans of the stewed tomatoes and the onion soup mix. Puree the contents of the third can of tomatoes and add to the mixture. Heat to boiling, then reduce heat and simmer for two hours. About a half hour before serving, add zucchini, mushrooms and garlic powder. Continue to simmer until dinner. Serve over rice or pasta. Makes 4-6 servings.

Bulgogee

If you can find a Korean specialty food shop, this recipe is for you. It calls for a particular cut of meat called bulgogee, which is somewhat similar to round steak. If you can't find bulgogee meat, you can use tenderized, pounded, round steak. The texture will be slightly different, but if you or your guests have never tasted bulgogee, who will know?

    4   garlic cloves, minced
    2   green onions, chopped (including tops)
    1   pound bulgogee meat, cut in 3 strips
    3   tablespoons sesame oil
    5   tablespoons soy sauce
  1/2   teaspoon pepper
    3   tablespoons sugar
    1   tablespoon sesame seeds

Mix all ingredients together. Marinate meat for 12 hours in covered bowl in refrigerator. When ready to cook, heat a little oil in a large frying pan and spread meat out in pan. Brown on both sides (about 5 minutes on each side). Makes 4 servings.

Stuffed Cabbage Rolls

According to Ceil Rosen, this is one of Moishe's favorite dishes. Please note Ceil's special hints at the end of the recipe. If you knew Ceil like we know Ceil, you'd really love her. In the meantime, try her recipe; you'll love it.

1	large head cabbage	1/4	cup grated onion
1 1/2	pounds ground beef	1 1/2	teaspoons salt
2/3	cup wheat germ or bread	1/8	teaspoon pepper
	crumbs	1/2	teaspoon garlic powder
1	cup milk		
2	eggs, beaten		

Sauce:
    2   (10 1/2-ounce) cans condensed tomato soup
  1-2   (16-ounce) cans whole cranberry sauce
    2   (8-ounce) cans tomato sauce
    1   tablespoon lemon juice

Wash, core and place a whole cabbage in a large pot, cored side up. Pour boiling water into hollow center and all around cabbage to cover. Cover and let stand 20 to 30 minutes until cabbage is pliant enough to pull off leaves without tearing them.

While cabbage is cooking, prepare sauce: Place all sauce ingredients in large saucepan and cook, stirring occasionally, over medium heat until well-blended. Remove from heat.

Meanwhile, mix ground beef, wheat germ, milk, eggs and seasonings. When leaves are pliant, remove one at a time and fill by placing 1 to 2 tablespoons of the meat mixture toward the base of each leaf (the amount of meat will depend on the size of the leaf). Roll the bottom of the leaf over the meat mixture, then fold in both sides simultaneously and roll up the rest of the way. There should be enough of the tip to tuck back into the roll so that it will not come apart during cooking. If leaves are not pliant enough, let individual leaves stand in hot water for 5-10 minutes more. Roll up all the larger leaves and shred the remaining cabbage as if for coleslaw.

Placed shredded cabbage in a large pot, sprinkle with salt to taste. Place cabbage rolls firmly side by side in one layer (if possible). Cover cabbage rolls with some of the sauce. Add another layer of cabbage rolls and continue to alternate with sauce. Cover pot and simmer 1 1/2 hours. There will be a considerable amount of soup. This can be served separately as sweet and sour cabbage soup, or you can serve the cabbage rolls in soup bowls. Makes 18 cabbage rolls.

Helpful hints: If the cabbage leaves are not pliable enough after the hot water treatment, gently shave off about half of the white spine at the base of the leaf. Form the meat mixture into cylindrical shapes and place them the wide way on the cabbage leaf. When rolling them up, press firmly to squeeze out excess moisture, and they will retain their shape better while cooking. Keep the heat low while cooking, so the sauce will not stick to the bottom of the pan.

Pasta e Piselli (Pasta with Peas)

Is there someone in your life who is your other mother? This recipe comes from Sandra Phillips, my other (Italian) mother. Sandra says that the trick to making this recipe correctly is to retain some of the cooking water with the pasta. Reserve about two cups of the pasta-water to be added as necessary. This recipe is a cross between a soup and a stew, leaning a little more to the soupy side.

Italians and Jews do seem to have a lot in common, especially when it comes to cooking. The Italian mother encourages, "Mangia, mangia!" (eat, eat); the Jewish mother urges, "Ess, ess!" (eat, eat). In any language, "eat, eat" is an encouragement to enjoy, so enjoy, enjoy this Pasta e Piselli.

1	pound ground beef
1	egg
2	slices white bread
	salt and pepper to taste
1/2	teaspoon garlic powder
1/4	cup grated Parmesan cheese
1	large onion, chopped
1/4	cup olive oil
2	(15-ounce) cans tomato sauce
1/2	teaspoon basil
1	(10-ounce) package frozen green peas
1	pound pasta shells

Mix meat, egg, bread, salt, pepper, garlic powder and Parmesan cheese together in a large mixing bowl.
Form mixture into tiny meatballs. In a medium-sized pot, sauté chopped onion in $1/4$ cup olive oil.
When onion is soft, add tomato sauce.
After 10 minutes, add meatballs to the sauce and let simmer for 45 minutes.
Add basil and peas during the last 10 minutes of cooking time.

About $1/2$ hour before serving, boil shells in slightly salted water.
Three minutes before shells are cooked, pour off water but leave a little soupy.
Do not drain.
Add meatball and sauce mixture to shells; let cook three minutes more.
Add more cooking water as necessary for desired consistency.
Makes 8-10 servings.

Enjoy!

Greek Hamburgers

The Yiddish word for grandmother is *bubba*. The Greek name is Yia Yia.

2	pounds ground beef
1	pound ground lamb
1	large onion, chopped
	olive oil
$1/2$	cup bread crumbs
2	eggs
4	tablespoons dried mint leaves
3	tablespoons dried oregano
1	teaspoon garlic powder
	salt and pepper to taste

In a large mixing bowl, mix together both types of meat.
In a medium skillet, sauté the onion in a tablespoon of olive oil over medium heat until limp.
Set aside and let cool.

Combine meat with the bread crumbs, eggs, mint, oregano, garlic powder and salt and pepper.
Mix in the cooled onions.
Cover and refrigerate at least two hours to blend the flavors.

Shape the meat mixture into small patties and place on a preheated broiler pan.
Broil a few minutes on both sides until desired level of cooking has been reached.
Makes 18 small burgers.

L.W.W. Beef Burgundy

This dish was cooked and served by Joel Kleinbaum at a farewell dinner for one of The Liberated Wailing Wall teams, as they were leaving for yet another deputation tour.

1 1/2	pounds beef stew meat, cut in bite-size cubes
1	medium onion, diced fine
1	medium carrot, diced fine
1	rib celery, diced fine
	about 2 dozen pearl onions (frozen or fresh), peeled*
6-8	mushrooms, sliced
	red cooking wine
	beef bouillon
2-3	tablespoons flour
	salt and pepper
	oil
1	bay leaf
1/4	teaspoon thyme
2	teaspoons chopped parsley
1-2	teaspoons tomato paste
1 or 2	cloves garlic, mashed

Dredge the meat in flour and sprinkle it with salt and pepper.

Heat some oil in a Dutch oven and sauté the onions, carrots and celery over medium heat until they soften.

Add the meat and brown it over medium high heat.

Pour off the fat and add the cooking wine and bouillon (one part bouillon to two parts cooking wine) until the beef is barely covered with liquid.

Add the bay leaf, thyme, parsley, tomato paste and mashed garlic.

Bring to a boil, cover and turn the heat down so it simmers gently.

After 2 hours the meat should be tender and the gravy thickened.

While the meat is simmering, brown the pearl onions gently in margarine or butter, without breaking the outer layers of the onion.

Set the onions aside and sauté the mushrooms in the same pot.

About 20-30 minutes before serving time,

add the mushrooms and onions to the meat mixture and heat slowly.

Makes 6 servings.

*To peel the onions, drop them in boiling water for a few seconds,

then drain immediately and cover with cold water.

The skins should slip off easily.

Cholent

Without a doubt, this is the traditional Jewish dish. Pronounced chu-lint, it is prepared by Jewish housewives on Friday afternoons before sundown and allowed to cook in a slow oven until lunch time on Saturday. This enables observant Jews to have a hot meal on Saturdays without lighting a fire once Sabbath has begun on Friday night. However, Jews and Gentiles can enjoy this dish anytime, that is, any time your oven happens to be free for 24 hours! Or use this version, which only requires three hours of cooking time.

1	package dried pinto beans
3/4	cup pearl barley
4	cloves garlic, minced or crushed
1-2	strips beef flanken, cut up (optional)
3	chicken bouillon cubes
	pepper

Mix all ingredients together in ovenproof casserole. Cover with 1" water. Cook about 3 hours in 350° oven. Makes 6-8 servings.

Brisket in Beer

The alcohol in the beer cooks off as the brisket bakes, leaving only the tender, moist, delicious beef.

3-4	pounds beef brisket (first cut is best)
1	can beer
	celery leaves to sprinkle on top
1/2	bottle chili sauce

Place brisket in a roasting pan. Sprinkle with celery leaves. Pour on chili sauce and beer. Place, uncovered, in 325° oven for 1 hour. Cover, lower oven to 225° and bake 3 more hours. Baste occasionally and check liquid, adding water if necessary. Makes 8-10 servings.

Milanesas

This recipe comes from an old, tattered Argentine cookbook that belongs to Zhava Glaser. She said her mother refused to part with the cookbook when their family came from Argentina to the United States. By that time the cookbook had lost its front cover and its brown, fragile pages were held together by brittle scotchtape. Zhava translated this recipe for us.

"Take a pound of round steak and have the butcher cut it into thin fillets. Flatten them a little and add salt and pepper. Beat two eggs and dip the fillets in them, then coat with bread crumbs (you can add garlic and oregano to the crumbs). Fry the fillets in very hot oil, about 1/4 cup, until they're nicely browned. Serve with a wedge of lemon." Makes 3-4 servings.

Zhava's note: These go well with freshly mashed potatoes made with plenty of milk and margarine.

Sabbath Burgers

One of the Jewish traditions that Lyn and Alan Bond enjoy is their Friday night dinner with their children. The Sabbath candles on the table make even the simplest of dinners seem more dramatic. Hamburgers are a favorite in their family (with two children, what would be more appropriate?). On Friday nights this dressed-up version is known as Sabbath Burgers.

1	pound lean ground beef
1	envelope onion soup mix
1/2	cup uncooked oats
1	slightly beaten egg
1/3	cup double strength beef bouillon (2 cubes dissolved in hot water)
1/3	cup cooking burgundy (if none is available, double the amount of bouillon)

Mix all ingredients together in large bowl. Form into six patties and broil approximately 5 minutes on each side. Makes 6 patties.

Veal Marsala

4	veal chops or 1 pound of veal cutlets or stewing veal
1/2	cup white wine vinegar
2	large onions, sliced thin
2	cloves garlic, minced
1	egg, beaten
1	cup bread crumbs
1/2	cup cooking marsala (optional)
1	cup beef broth (if you eliminate the marsala, add 1/2 cup more broth)

Place veal in a bowl and cover with wine vinegar. Allow to marinate about 1 hour. In a frying pan, sauté the onion and the garlic; when lightly browned, remove to a bowl. Dip veal in egg, then in bread crumbs. Fry until golden brown. Add garlic and onions to meat in pan and cover all with liquid. Bring to a simmer. Cook for 1 hour, turning occasionally. Makes 4 servings.

Sweet and Sour Tongue

Before you say "ugh!" please try this recipe. Tongue is one of those underrated cuts of meat that few seem to understand. In many Jewish homes it is standard fare, and really is quite delicious.

1	8-ounce can tomato sauce
1/2	cup lemon juice
1/4	cup water
2/3	cup raisins
1/2	cup brown sugar
1	fully cooked beef tongue, sliced thin (allow about 1/4-pound per person, at least)

Combine all ingredients in a large pot and bring to a boil. Reduce heat and simmer for 1 hour. Serve over rice.

Say it Again, Veal Marsala

- 2 ounces olive oil
- 8 tablespoons butter or margarine
- 4 thick veal loin chops
   flour to coat veal
   salt and pepper
- 1/2 pound mushrooms, sliced
- 1 cup cooking Marsala wine
- 2 ounces chicken or beef bouillon
- 1 teaspoon flour

Heat oil and 2 tablespoons of the butter or margarine in a large frying pan until melted.

Dip veal chops in flour to coat; sauté veal slowly in oil/butter mixture until richly browned on both sides.

Meanwhile, in small saucepan, melt 2 tablespoons butter or margarine and brown mushrooms slowly.

Add cooking Marsala, bouillon and remaining 4 tablespoons butter or margarine, plus 1 teaspoon flour; heat over low flame until slightly thickened and smooth.

When veal is cooked, pour mushroom sauce over top and serve.

Makes 4 servings.

Pot Roast

- 2 large onions, chopped fine
- 2 tablespoons dried oregano
- 2 bay leaves, whole
- 1/4 cup catsup
- 1/2 cup water
- 2 pounds beef top round steak or chuck roast

Place all ingredients in a Dutch oven, making sure meat is just covered by liquid.

If more liquid is needed, add equal parts catsup and water.

Bring to a boil, then lower heat and simmer, covered, for 1 hour over very low heat.

Remove meat and slice thin; return meat to cooking liquid and continue to cook over low heat for one hour, or until tender.

Allow to cool and refrigerate overnight.

Skim hardened fat from top and reheat over low flame.

Makes 4-6 servings.

Beef with Knaidle (Dumplings)

- 1   pound short ribs or beef brisket
- 12   carrots, peeled and grated
- 3   sweet potatoes, peeled and diced
- $1/2$ cup honey
-     salt and pepper

Combine all ingredients in an ovenproof Dutch oven. Add enough water to cover and simmer on stovetop until carrots and potatoes are almost tender (about 1 $1/2$ hours). Make knaidle and place them close to the meat, cover pan and continue simmering for 20 minutes or until knaidle expand. Finish in a 350° oven for 30 minutes or until thick and brown. Makes 6 servings.

Knaidle:
- 1   cup flour
- $1/4$ teaspoon baking powder
- $1/4$ teaspoon salt
- 1   tablespoon sugar
- 2   tablespoons margarine
- 3   tablespoons cold water

Sift dry ingredients, cut in margarine and add water slowly until a soft ball of dough is formed. Roll between wet hands into walnut-sized dumplings.

Mitch Glaser's Favorite Filet Mignon

It's not that Mitch Glaser is such a classy guy that he insists on eating high-caliber delicacies like filet mignon. But this dish was created especially for our beloved missionary by another Mitch, Mr. Forman. Mr. Glaser has a reputation for putting catsup on everything—even ice cream and chicken soup. We know that there is something wrong with this behavior, but we're willing to put up with it because he is such a good missionary with a heart for the Lord. However, he dare not come near Mr. Forman's creation with a bottle of that red stuff.

- 4   filet mignon steaks, 8 ounces each
- 4   red bell peppers
- 1   ounce chopped garlic
-     the juice of one lemon (about 3 tablespoons)

To make the sauce, wash the bell peppers and roast them over an open flame until the peppers turn black, turning occasionally (under a broiler flame works well). When they are all roasted, put them in a clean brown paper bag, close the bag and let them sit for $1/2$ hour. When they are cool, you should be able to peel off the skin. Remove the seeds. Puree the peppers, garlic and lemon juice in a blender until silky smooth.

Saute the steaks in a frying pan until they are medium rare, about 7 minutes on each side. Top each steak with some catsup. . .um, we mean, red pepper sauce. Makes 4 servings.

Barbecued Steak

1	cup catsup
1/2	cup water
1/4	cup vinegar
1/4	cup green pepper, chopped
1/4	cup onion, chopped
1 1/2	tablespoons Worcestershire sauce
1	tablespoon mustard
2	tablespoons brown sugar
1/2	teaspoon salt
1/8	teaspoon pepper
4	pounds round steak, cut 1/2" thick

Combine all ingredients except round steak in saucepan.
Bring to a boil, then simmer gently about 5 minutes.
Pound steak; cut it into serving-size portions.
Place pieces in a large roaster.
Pour sauce over meat.
Cover and bake at 325° for 1 1/2-2 hours.
Makes 8 servings.

Spaghetti with Veal in Tomato Sauce

2	tablespoons olive or vegetable oil
2 1/2	pounds boned veal shoulder, cut into 1-inch cubes
10	garlic cloves, minced
2	cups canned tomato sauce
2/3	cup Marsala cooking wine
1/2	teaspoon dried rosemary leaves, crushed
	salt and pepper to taste
1	pound spaghetti, cooked

In 3 or 4 quart saucepan heat oil over medium heat; add veal and sauté, turning frequently, until lightly browned on all sides.
Reduce heat to low, add garlic cloves, and continue to sauté for 2 more minutes.
Add remaining ingredients, except spaghetti, stirring well.
Cover and let simmer, stirring occasionally, until veal is tender, about 1-1 1/2 hours.
Serve over spaghetti.
Makes 6 servings.

Stuffed Cabbage, Greek Style

1	large head cabbage
2	onions, chopped
1	clove garlic, chopped
2	tablespoons butter or margarine
1	pound ground beef
1	cup rice, raw
1/2	teaspoon oregano
1	tablespoon minced fresh parsley (or 1/2 teaspoon dried)
1	tablespoon minced fresh mint (or 1/2 teaspoon dried)
1/4	teaspoon cinnamon
1/2	cup water
2	cups beef broth
1	(15-ounce) can tomato sauce

Prepare cabbage: Remove core of cabbage. Boil large pot of water to cover cabbage; plunge into boiling water. Parboil for 5 minutes; turn heat to low and simmer, uncovered, for 5 minutes more. Remove cabbage from pot; drain; separate into 25-30 leaves when cool enough to handle. Chop leftover leaves and line bottom of large Dutch oven with chopped cabbage.

Prepare filling: Brown chopped onions and garlic in butter or margarine. Add spices and rice and brown meat well. Mixture should be soft; add a small amount of water if it isn't. Mix thoroughly.

Place one tablespoon of filling along wide edge of each cabbage leaf. Turn in ends and roll leaf. Arrange rolls, edges down, in medium baking pan. Sprinkle with salt and pepper. Add beef broth, tomato sauce and enough water to cover rolls. Weigh rolls down with heavy dish. Cover and simmer one hour over low flame, adding water if necessary. Makes 6-8 servings.

Stuffed Grape Leaves with Avgolemono Sauce

Use the preceding recipe with the following substitutions:

Substitute 1 pound jar of grapevine leaves for the cabbage leaves. Follow same method, omitting tomato sauce. (Optional: add 1/2 teaspoon dried dillweed to stuffing). Cover bottom of greased Dutch oven with washed, torn grape leaves. Stuff leaves with shiny side to the outside.

Avgolemono sauce: With electric mixer, beat 3 egg whites until stiff. Add 3 egg yolks and continue beating. Slowly add the juice of 1-2 lemons, beating constantly so sauce does not curdle. Dissolve 1 tablespoon cornstarch in a little cold water. Add to this 1 cup chicken broth. Add mixture slowly to egg-lemon mixture, beating constantly. Sauce should be smooth and creamy. Check seasoning; add salt and pepper if necessary. Sauce can be made ahead and reheated in double boiler. Do not cook sauce with grapevine rolls, but serve separately, as sauce may curdle if it becomes too hot. Spoon over rolls when done.

Imitation Gefilte Fish (Made with Veal)

3/4   pound ground veal
1   small onion, grated
1   egg
1   tablespoon matzoh meal or flour
     salt and pepper to taste
1   large onion, diced
1   carrot
3   potatoes

Mix ground veal with grated onion, egg, matzoh meal or flour, and salt and pepper to taste. In large casserole dish, greased, place diced large onion and slice carrots over onion. Shape meat into 4 small loaves and put them on top of carrots. Add quartered potatoes, 2 cups of water and salt and pepper to taste. Cover and bake at 350° for 1 hour or until done. Makes 4-6 servings

Macaroni and Hamburger

1   pound ground beef
1   onion, chopped
1   clove garlic, minced
1   (15-ounce) can tomato sauce
     dash ground cloves
     dash ground cinnamon
1   pound cooked macaroni

Brown ground beef with onion and garlic in large frying pan (no oil necessary). Add tomato sauce, cloves and cinnamon and simmer over low heat until well-blended. Serve over cooked macaroni in this manner: Brown a little butter in small frying pan; pour this over macaroni; pour sauce over this and add a little grated Parmesan cheese. Makes 4 servings.

Shirley's Meat Dish

This recipe is from Cecilia Butcher's friend Shirley who attends Highline Christian Church in Seattle.

1   pound ground beef
1   onion, chopped
1   egg
1/4   cup bread crumbs
1   tablespoon Dijon mustard
1   tablespoon ground cumin
1   teaspoon lemon pepper
1/4   cup fresh parsley, chopped

Mix all ingredients together. Form into balls about the size of walnuts. Brown in frying pan until cooked through. Mixture can also be made into a loaf and baked at 350° for 1 hour. Makes 4 servings.

Lamb Shanks

This dish is a favorite of Cecilia Butcher's mother.

4	lamb shanks
4	ounces tomato sauce
2	medium onions
2	tablespoons parsley, minced
1/2	cup red cooking wine
	garlic powder
	salt and pepper to taste

Place lamb shanks in a roasting pan; combine remaining ingredients and pour over shanks to cover. Bake 1½ hours, covered, at 350°. Do not undercook or meat will be tough. Whole, peeled potatoes may be cooked with the shanks; they will absorb the liquid. Makes 4 servings.

Lamb Ribs, Sorta Barbecued

	lamb ribs, about 1/2-1 pound per person
3/4	cup catsup
3/4	cup water
2	medium onions, chopped
2	tablespoons brown sugar
3	tablespoons Worcestershire sauce
1	tablespoon apple cider vinegar
	salt and pepper to taste

Mix together all ingredients except lamb ribs in bowl. Pour over ribs in large frying pan or Dutch oven (with cover). Bring to a boil, lower heat and simmer, covered, for 1½ hours. Skim off fat. This dish can be refrigerated overnight. Skim off fat next day. Serve with rice. Sauce is sufficient to cover 4 pounds of ribs.

Mediterranean Rack of Lamb

2	racks of lamb (8 ribs each)
2	ounces Dijon mustard
4	ounces seasoned breadcrumbs
4	ounces Kalamata olives
4	ounces roasted red peppers (jar)
4	ounces capers
4	ounces cornichon pickles
1/4	bunch fresh mint
2	ounces balsamic vinegar
1/2	ounce garlic, chopped

Rub mustard all along the back side of each rack of lamb. Dip each rack into seasoned breadcrumbs, pressing along sides. Preheat oven to 375° and cook the lamb until medium rare (140°). Remove from oven and let stand for 1/2 hour. In small bowl, place pitted olives and remaining ingredients (except the mint); chop fine. Chop the mint separately and add to olive mixture. Mix all together well. Take the rack of lamb and cut down through each rib, so that you have 16 separate chops. Serve 4 chops per person and cover with the relish. Makes 4 servings.

Landrum's Lamb in Coconut Milk

Rahel Landrum was not at all sheepish about giving us this unusual recipe.

1 1/2	pounds ground lamb
1	lemon
2	teaspoons salt
1	(450 ml.) can coconut milk
	cooking oil
1 1/2	large onions, chopped
2	cloves garlic, chopped
1/2	teaspoon ground ginger
2	teaspoons ground cumin
2	teaspoons paprika
1/2	teaspoon pepper
1	(4-ounce) can tomato puree
1	teaspoon salt

One day ahead:

Squeeze the lemon juice over the meat; add the salt and coconut milk. Marinate, covered, in the refrigerator for 24 hours.

In large frying pan, over medium heat, cook the chopped onions in the oil until soft. Add garlic; cook 2 minutes. Add ginger. Add meat and simmer, covered, for 15 minutes. Remove meat, add the rest of the spices and the tomato puree. Stir and add a little water if it's too dry. Cook for 2 minutes. Add the meat once again, stirring constantly, and simmer, covered, until the meat is tender, about 15 minutes. Makes 6 servings.

Mae's Summer Hamburger Dish

1	pound ground beef
3	zucchini, sliced
1	onion, sliced
1	clove garlic, minced

Brown ground beef in large frying pan; add remaining ingredients and simmer over low heat until all is soft and browned. Serve with French bread. Makes 4 servings.

Veal Dumplings with Pasta

1   pound ground veal
1   cup fresh bread crumbs
$1/2$ cup green onions, finely chopped
$1/2$ cup parsley, finely chopped
1   clove garlic, chopped
1   egg, lightly beaten
$1 \, 1/4$ teaspoons salt
$1/2$ teaspoon pepper

Fresh tomato sauce:
2   tablespoons butter or margarine
1   (28-ounce) can Italian plum tomatoes, drained, seeded and chopped
2   cloves garlic, minced
    salt
2   tablespoons fresh basil, chopped
$1/2$ pound cooked spaghetti, macaroni or capellini
1   cup Parmesan cheese, grated

In large bowl place veal, crumbs, green onions, parsley, garlic, egg, salt and pepper.
Mix to blend well and form into one-inch balls.
Drop veal balls into large pot of boiling water and cook over very high heat until balls float to top, 3-5 minutes.
Remove with slotted spoon to bowl.
Make sauce by melting butter or margarine in large saucepan; add canned tomatoes, garlic, salt and basil.
Simmer 10-15 minutes.
Place veal balls in sauce and simmer, covered, over low heat 10-15 minutes.
Pour over cooked pasta when done; sprinkle with grated Parmesan.
Makes 4-6 servings.

Nancy's Easy Beef Dish

1   pound ground beef
1   (16-ounce) package frozen mixed vegetables
1   (10 $1/2$-ounce) can condensed cream of mushroom soup

Brown beef in a large frying pan until it is no longer red.
Drain off fat.
Add remaining ingredients; bring to a boil, lower heat and simmer, covered, until vegetables are heated through (about 10 minutes).
Makes 4-6 servings.

Meatball and Eggplant Casserole

1 1/2	pounds ground chuck		1/4	cup olive oil
3/4	cup seasoned bread crumbs		1	medium-size eggplant
1	small onion, minced		1/3	cup flour
3/4	teaspoon cornstarch		1/4	teaspoon salt
1	egg, beaten		1	cup olive oil
3/4	cup light cream		1	(8-ounce) package mozzarella cheese, shredded
3/4	teaspoon salt		2	(15-ounce) cans tomato sauce
			1/2	teaspoon oregano

Mix first 7 ingredients together in large bowl; shape into walnut-size balls and brown in olive oil in large frying pan.
Slice eggplant into 1/2" slices, coat with flour and salt.
Sauté in vegetable oil until golden, about 5-7 minutes on each side.

In large casserole or baking pan layer half of eggplant, meatballs, cheese and tomato sauce.
Sprinkle with half of the oregano, then repeat with remainder of ingredients, ending with oregano.

Bake uncovered for 1 hour at 350°. Let stand for 10 minutes before serving. Makes 4-6 servings.

Mediterranean Stew

2	pounds stewing beef, cut in 1"cubes		1	(8-ounce) can mushroom pieces, drained
2	tablespoons cooking oil		2	tablespoons cornstarch
1	cup sliced onion		1 1/2	cups canned tomatoes
1	green pepper, cut in 1" strips		2	teaspoons salt
1/2	cup celery, sliced		1/4	teaspoon pepper
			4-6	potatoes, peeled and quartered

Brown meat in oil.
Place meat in the bottom of a 2 1/2 quart casserole.
Layer onion, green pepper, celery and mushrooms over meat.
Dissolve cornstarch in a little water, blend into tomatoes and bring mixture to a boil, stirring constantly; stir in salt and pepper.
Pour thickened tomato sauce over casserole.
Place potatoes on top of sauce. Cover and bake at 350° for 2 1/2 hours.
Makes 6 servings.

Pot Roast Deluxe

2 tablespoons butter or margarine
3 onions, sliced thin
2 cloves garlic, minced
3 pounds boneless beef chuck
$1/2$ cup water
1 teaspoon salt
$1/8$ teaspoon ginger
$1/4$ teaspoon pepper
1 ounce dried mushrooms
1 cup prunes, pitted
1 cup hot water

In Dutch oven, melt butter or margarine and sauté onions and garlic until lightly browned over medium heat. Add meat and cook until brown on all sides. Add water and seasonings. Cover and simmer over low heat for $1^{1}/2$ hours. While the meat is cooking, soak the mushrooms and prunes in 1 cup hot water. Add them (with the water) after the meat has cooked. Simmer for an additional $1/2$ hour. Serve the meat on a platter with the prunes and mushrooms around it. Makes 8-10 servings

Osso Buco

Don't worry if you can't pronounce this, just call it whatever you like. Another good name for this dish could be "When You're Done, Eat the Marrow," but then, nobody would know what you're talking about! Actually, this is a very French beef recipe that came from Daphna, an Israeli believer in Jesus.

$1/2$ cup flour
8 pieces of osso buco meat (ask your butcher)
4 tablespoons olive oil
2 cloves garlic, chopped
1 onion, finely chopped
6 tomatoes, peeled and chopped
4 tablespoons fresh parsley, finely chopped
salt and pepper
$1/2$ cup red cooking wine

Put the flour in a plastic bag; drop in the pieces of meat and shake until well-floured. In a large skillet, heat 2 tablespoons olive oil and brown the pieces of meat on all sides until well-browned. Remove the meat and wipe out the skillet with paper towels. Add remaining 2 tablespoons olive oil, heat over medium flame; add garlic and onion, and sauté for a few minutes. Add tomatoes and half the parsley; cook together, stirring for 5 minutes. Return the meat to the skillet; add salt and pepper, and the cooking wine. Bring to a boil; cover and cook over very low heat for 1 $1/2$ hours. Before serving, remove cover and add remaining parsley. Cook, uncovered, for 5 more minutes. Makes 6-8 servings.

Note: It is customary and acceptable to eat, with great gusto, the marrow from the center of the bones when you are finished devouring the meat.

Norwegian Hot Dish

Maggie Reed is the charming wife of Russ, a member of the Jews for Jesus Board of Directors. She told us, with a little laugh, the story behind this recipe. It seems that in the early days of their courtship, Maggie submitted recipes to local newspapers, who offered a small amount of money for their readers who sent in recipes. This Norwegian Hot Dish earned Maggie a small sum - and perhaps that's why Russ married her! We smile along with Maggie, who says this is a good family dish for cold, winter nights; it can also be doubled or tripled to feed a large crowd.

2-3	tablespoons oil
1	onion, chopped
1	pound lean ground beef
$1/4$	teaspoon pepper
1	(15-ounce can) red kidney beans
1	(10 $1/2$-ounce) can condensed tomato soup
3-4	sliced, raw potatoes (sliced thin)
	a little paprika, if desired

Heat the oil in a large skillet over medium heat; add the onion and ground beef, and brown well. Add the beans, soup and potatoes; mix together well. Pour into an ovenproof casserole and bake at 350° for 1 hour. Makes 4-6 servings.

Chicken, the Jewish Bird

What are your childhood memories made of? Ours are about chicken. Chicken fricassee, roast chicken, baked chicken, chopped chicken liver, boiled chicken with noodles. Some of us could eat chicken everyday, and do! That's the way it is in many Jewish homes. Years ago, each Jewish neighborhood had its own little chicken stand right on the street, where housewives could pick out a chicken and have it killed and plucked fresh. What a squawking must have been heard.

Talking about chicken always reminds me of a funny-but-true story told by Pat Boker, a former art director for Jews for Jesus. It's an un-recipe for chicken tacos, otherwise known as the trick to getting two birds from one pot. The story goes like this: One day, Pat was showing Amy (a former office manager at our Headquarters) how to make chicken tacos. The first step was to boil a chicken in a large pot of water. Amy asked Pat, "What do you do with the water after you cook the chicken?" Pat replied, "Oh, I just spill it down the drain." Amy shrieked (she was famous for shrieking), "But that's how you make chicken soup!" Needless to say, from that day on Pat thought twice about wasting that precious chicken-water whenever she made chicken tacos.

Jewish Roast Chicken

Very simple, very garlicky, very good and very Jewish, as are most things made with garlic. This is guaranteed to make your home smell Jewish!

1   roasting chicken, about 3 pounds, cut up into serving-size pieces
     garlic powder
     paprika
     margarine or butter
     salt and pepper

Rinse chicken and pat dry with paper towels. Sprinkle heavily with garlic powder, paprika, salt and pepper to taste. Cut small bits of margarine or butter and smear them all over the chicken. Roast in roasting pan at 325° for 1½-2 hours or until done, basting occasionally with pan juices. Makes 4-6 servings.

Chicken Kapama

Submitted by a Greek friend, Georgie, this dish is unusual because the sauce is made with a clove-studded onion. Be sure to use lots of cloves (this recipe calls for a dozen, but two dozen are better), even though your fingers will suffer for it as you push them into the onion.

2   tablespoons butter or margarine
1   (2½-3 pound) frying chicken, cut up
        salt and pepper
        oregano
2   tablespoons butter or margarine
1   (8-ounce) can tomato sauce
2   tablespoons tomato paste
1   medium onion
12-15   whole cloves
1   pound spaghetti, cooked

Melt butter or margarine in a large frying pan.
Sprinkle salt, pepper and oregano to taste on chicken.
Sauté the chicken slowly in the melted butter or margarine.
While chicken is browning, put the tomato sauce in a 3-quart saucepan.
Dilute the tomato paste with 2 ounces of hot water and add this to the tomato sauce.
Peel the onion and push the cloves into it, placing the cloves all over the onion.
Put the onion in the saucepan.
When the chicken is browned, put it in the saucepan.
Mix the remaining butter left in the frying pan with the flour and put this mixture into the saucepan.
Bring to a boil. Lower heat and simmer, covered, for one hour. Serve with spaghetti.
Makes 4 servings.

Lemon Chicken

    1   cup lemon juice
    5   cloves garlic, crushed
    2   tablespoons soy or teriyaki sauce
    1   (3 ½ pound) frying chicken, cut into serving pieces

Place lemon juice, crushed garlic and teriyaki or soy sauce in a large bowl; mix well. Add chicken pieces and allow them to marinate in refrigerator, covered, for three or four days (the chicken will not spoil as the lemon juice acts as a preservative). Remove chicken from the marinade and place chicken pieces in large baking dish; pour marinade over all. Bake at 350° for one hour. Makes 4 servings. Serve with Lemon Parsley Rice.

Lemon Parsley Rice

Follow cooking directions on the box of rice, substituting ¼ cup lemon juice for ¼ cup of water for each 2 cups of cooked rice. When rice is cooked, toss with 1-2 tablespoons of dried parsley. Makes 4 servings.

Easy and Delicious Chicken with Rice

    1   tablespoon vegetable oil
    1   (3 ½ pound) frying chicken, cut up
    1   onion, chopped
 1 ½   cups rice, uncooked
        salt and pepper to taste

Heat oil in large frying pan. Brown chicken and onions over medium heat. Add water to cover, bring to boil and simmer, covered, for 10-15 minutes. Add rice, cover and cook for 20-30 minutes more, adding more water if necessary to cook rice. Season to taste with salt and pepper (about 1 teaspoon salt, ¼ teaspoon pepper). Makes 4 servings.

Kathleen's Chicken and Broccoli

    3   pounds chicken breasts (not boneless)
    1   pound broccoli
    1   cup mayonnaise (can be low-calorie or fat-free)
    2   (10 ½-ounce) cans cream of chicken soup
    1   teaspoon curry powder
 1 ½   teaspoons lemon juice
    1   package bread stuffing mix (enough for 10 pounds of poultry)
   ¼   cup butter or margarine

Boil chicken in small amount of water to cover until done (about 1 hour). Cool chicken and tear into bite-size pieces, discarding skin and bones. This can be done a day ahead. Grease 9"x13" baking dish and arrange chicken pieces in it. Chop broccoli into bite-sized pieces, and sprinkle them over the chicken. To make the sauce, mix together mayonnaise, soup, curry powder and lemon juice in bowl. Pour sauce over chicken and broccoli. Bake at 350° for 20 minutes. Remove from oven and sprinkle stuffing crumbs on top; melt margarine or butter and pour it over the crumbs. Bake an additional 15 minutes. Makes 4-6 servings.

Renee's Baked Breast of Chicken

Please note that Renee's name is spelled with two e's, not one. Mrs. Renee Abend is a Jewish believer who lives and cooks in New York City. This is one of her famous recipes, which is unbelievably easy to fix and equally unbelievably fabulous to eat.

4	whole chicken breasts, boned
1	cup flour (or for Passover, matzoh meal)
1	teaspoon ginger
1	teaspoon garlic powder
1/2	teaspoon salt
1/4	teaspoon white pepper
1	egg, well beaten
1	cup apricot preserves
1/2	cup white cooking wine
1	tablespoon margarine

Cut chicken breasts in half, rinse and pat dry with paper towels. Combine flour (or matzoh meal) with spices on a piece of waxed paper. Dip breasts in egg wash and then in flour (matzoh meal) coating. Arrange breasts in a single layer in a greased baking dish. Combine preserves, cooking wine and margarine in a small saucepan; cook over low heat until melted. Pour over chicken breasts and bake at 350° for 1 hour. Makes 6-8 servings.

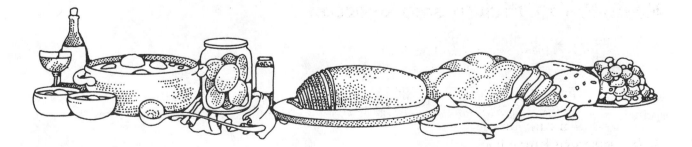

Chicken with Fruit Sauce (Lowfat and Sugar-free)

Lauren Kretzer, a Jewish balabusta (accomplished homemaker and cook) in Queens, New York, submitted this recipe. It is especially good served over rice.

- 6 boneless chicken breast halves (with skin on)
- 2 (16-ounce) cans sliced or halved peaches in juice
- 1 (6-ounce) can frozen orange juice concentrate
- 3 tablespoons all-fruit orange marmalade
- 1/2 tablespoon ginger
- 2 tablespoons soy sauce
- 1 tablespoon cornstarch mixed with 1/2 cup cold water
- 3 tablespoons raisins

Place chicken in a baking pan that has been sprayed with cooking spray. Bake at 400° for 30 minutes. While chicken is cooking, drain juice from peaches into a saucepan; set peaches aside. Add orange juice, marmalade, ginger and soy sauce to juice in pan. Heat until boiling; stir in cornstarch mixture and stir until thickened, about 2 minutes. Add reserved peaches and raisins. Remove chicken from baking pan; remove skin. Drain drippings from pan. Return chicken to pan and pour sauce over all. Return to oven for 15 minutes more. Makes 4-6 servings (about 290 calories each serving).

Melinda's Chicken Spaghetti

Melinda Tilles, wife of the handsome Jewish doctor, Steve, is one of the perkiest people we know. They live in High Point, North Carolina, where Melinda often makes this dish.

- 2 cups cooked, diced chicken
- 1/4 cup onion, chopped
- 1/4 cup green pepper, chopped
- 1/2 cup V-8 juice
- 1 (10 1/2-ounce) can cream of mushroom soup
- 1 1/2 cups sharp cheddar, grated
- 1/4 pound spaghetti, cooked and cut
- 3 fresh mushrooms
- 2 stalks celery, chopped
- 8 black pitted olives, sliced
- 1/2-1 cup chicken broth or bouillon
  garlic salt

Mix all ingredients together, using only half the grated cheddar cheese in the mixture. Reserve 3/4 cup to sprinkle over the top. Bake in a greased casserole at 350° for 50 minutes or until bubbly. Makes 4-6 servings.

Plum Chicken

1	(3-pound) chicken, cut into pieces
1	onion, sliced thin
1	clove garlic, crushed
$^2/_3$	cup plum preserves
1 $^1/_2$	teaspoons lemon juice
1 $^1/_2$	teaspoons Dijon mustard
1	(8-ounce) can crushed pineapple, in its own juice

In large frying pan or Dutch oven sauté onion and garlic in small amount of oil until soft; remove and set aside. Add chicken pieces to pan and cook over medium heat until tender and golden brown. Add sautéed onion and garlic along with remaining ingredients; bring to a boil. Cook over low heat until chicken is cooked, about 10 minutes. Makes 4-6 servings.

Mediterranean Chicken with Grilled Polenta Diamonds

1	chicken, about 3 pounds, quartered
2	(16-ounce) cans diced tomatoes, drained
6	cloves garlic
1	(8-ounce) jar green olives, drained
1	(8-ounce) jar pitted black olives, drained
2	ounces sundried tomatoes
4	ounces capers with juice
2	lemons, cut in half
8	ounces red cooking wine
1	teaspoon each fresh thyme, marjoram and oregano (or $^1/_4$ teaspoon dried of each)

Place chicken in roasting pan; cover with remaining ingredients.
Cover pan and bake 1 hour at 350°.
Turn heat up to 375°, remove cover and bake 15 minutes more.
Makes 4 servings.

Polenta Diamonds:

Make polenta according to package directions.
When it has cooked 40 minutes, add 4 ounces butter. Take one bunch fresh basil, chopped fine, and mix in.
Pour polenta into shallow baking dish, cover with plastic wrap and refrigerate.
When hard, remove from refrigerator and score into diamond pattern.
Take diamonds and grill individually on each side for two minutes. Put in oven at 375° for 10 minutes.
Take 2 red bell peppers, roast in oven for $^1/_2$ hour; cut into julienned strips, marinate in 4 ounces balsamic vinegar and 4 ounces olive oil.
Serve over baked polenta.

Baked Chicken Breasts with Fruit Curry Sauce

Moishe Rosen, who is not fond of chicken, devoured this dish at a Jews for Jesus Board of Directors meeting in the summer of 1990.

4 whole chicken breasts, boned

Marinade:
- 1/2   stem fresh ginger, sliced
- 4   ounces red wine vinegar
- 4   ounces olive oil
- 1/2   small red onion, chopped

Fruit curry sauce:
- 1/2   Granny Smith apple, diced
- 1   banana, sliced thin
- 2   ounces dried apricots
- 1   green pepper, diced
- 1/2   small red onion, diced
- 1/4   bunch fresh mint, chopped
- 1/4   bunch fresh basil, chopped
- 1/4   bunch fresh cilantro, chopped
- 2   ounces garlic, chopped
- 8   ounces heavy cream
- 4   ounces apple juice
- 2   ounces flour

Marinate the chicken overnight in shallow baking dish in refrigerator.

To make the fruit curry sauce, sauté in a medium size saucepan the garlic, apples, peppers and onions until soft. Add the flour and stir 1 minute.

Add the cream, apple juice, fresh herbs, bananas and apricots and simmer for 1 hour over very low heat. If the sauce gets too thick, add a little more apple juice.

Bake the chicken in the pan with the marinade in a preheated oven at 375°.

Cook until done, about 20 minutes.

To serve, pour the fruit curry sauce over the chicken.

Makes 4 servings.

Apricot Chicken Wheat Pilaf

6	chicken legs	$1/2$	cup raisins
6	chicken thighs		boiling water
1 $1/2$	teaspoons salt	$1/4$	cup margarine or butter
$1/2$	teaspoon cinnamon	2	cups onion, diced
$1/2$	teaspoon ground cumin	3	cups chicken broth
1	cup quartered dried apricots	1 $1/2$	cups bulgur wheat

Rinse chicken and pat dry. Rub spices into skin.

Place apricots and raisins in bowl; cover with boiling water. Melt margarine or butter in large pot.

Add half the chicken and cook five minutes on each side.

Cook remainder of chicken and remove from pot.

Add onion to skillet and cook 5 minutes, stirring constantly.

Add chicken broth and boil, scraping up brown bits from bottom of pot.

Return chicken and its juices to the skillet; add drained dried fruits on top of chicken.

Bring to a boil; cover and simmer for 10 minutes. Sprinkle bulgur wheat into skillet and push down into liquid.

Cover and simmer over low heat for about 20 minutes.   Serve from skillet.

Makes 6-8 servings.

Chicken in the Nest

- 2 cups cooked pasta, any type
- 2 chicken breasts, skinned, boned and cubed
- or 8 thighs, skinned, boned and cubed
- 1 onion, finely chopped
- $1/4$ cup olive oil
- $1/2$ pound fresh mushrooms
- $1/4$ cup Parmesan cheese, grated
- 1 cup plain yogurt
- $1/2$ cup cooking sherry (or $1/2$ cup water plus 1 chicken bouillon cube plus 2 tablespoons lemon juice)
- 2 chicken bouillon cubes dissolved in $1/2$ cup hot water
  pepper
  parsley and paprika for garnish

Heat oil in large pan and sauté onions until translucent.

Remove from pan and add chicken (adding more oil if necessary).

Sauté until just underdone.

Add the rest of the ingredients and cover; simmer 5-10 minutes until warmed through.

Sprinkle with parsley and paprika.

Makes 4 servings.

Orange Honey Chicken

1	(2 1/2-3 pound) frying chicken, cut in pieces
	salt and pepper
1-2	teaspoons dried tarragon
2	tablespoons butter or margarine
1	small onion
	the grated rind of 1 orange
	juice of 1 orange (plus 1/3 cup more orange juice)
2	tablespoons honey (more if you like)

Lightly salt and pepper the chicken and sprinkle with tarragon. Chop the onion. Melt the butter or margarine, add the onion to pan along with the orange rind. Coat the chicken with this mixture. Place the chicken in a baking dish, in one layer; pour the rest of the butter mixture over chicken. Bake at 425° until golden brown. Turn oven down to 325° and pour a little orange juice and/or water into the pan. Heat together slowly in a separate pan the rest of the orange juice, the honey and some of the pan juices. Coat the chicken well with this mixture. Cover with aluminum foil and bake until chicken is tender (total cooking time is about 1 hour). Makes 4 servings.

Orange Glazed Duck

1	duck, about 5 pounds
3	tablespoons margarine
1	medium onion, chopped fine
2	cups soft bread crumbs
1	egg, beaten
1/3	cup raisins
1/4	cup hot water
1/2	teaspoon salt
1/4	teaspoon pepper
1/4	teaspoon ground sage
1	tablespoon fresh parsley, minced

Sauce:

2	oranges, sliced thin, rind removed and grated, juice reserved
1/2	teaspoon cornstarch
	enough water to make one cup liquid

In large pot, melt margarine over low heat. Raise heat to medium and sauté onion until tender. Remove from heat and add bread crumbs, egg and raisins. Moisten with water and mix in salt, pepper, sage and parsley. Rinse duck inside and out and pat dry with paper towels. Stuff cavity with bread mixture. Roast, uncovered, at 325° for two hours. Pour off excess fat. Mix together ingredients for sauce in medium saucepan, bring to a boil and stir constantly until sauce thickens. Pour over duck and roast 1/2 hour more, or until duck is well-browned. Makes 6-8 servings.

Sharon's Mustard Chicken

Sharon Freeman is a Jewish believer who was born in Massachusetts, raised in California, and found the Lord while living in Hawaii. She is presently a full-time Jews for Jesus missionary living in Boston—quite a peripatetic woman!

chicken parts (at least 2 pieces per person)
1 small bottle lowfat Italian dressing
2-3 tablespoons horseradish mustard or spicy brown mustard

Combine salad dressing with enough mustard to make a spicy mixture (in Hawaii they say, "Da more mustard, da more spicy"). Place chicken pieces in casserole dish and pour marinade over all. Cover dish with aluminum foil and bake at 350° for 1 hour or until done. Serve with rice.

Note: Lawry's makes a great herb garlic marinade that works well in place of the Italian dressing.

Grebenes and Schmaltz

Moishe Rosen wanted this recipe included, even though you should only make it once a year and only after your cholesterol checks out okay! Though the name sounds like a comedy team from the Catskills, grebenes and schmaltz is actually a very tasty dish made of chicken skin that's been fried in rendered chicken fat. See what I mean about cholesterol? It's delicious but made to be eaten in small quantities, and only when you're feeling especially healthy.

	the skin of 1 chicken	1	small onion, diced
1	pound chicken fat (schmaltz)	$1/4$	cup water

Cut chicken skin and fat into one-inch squares. Place chicken fat, skin, onion and water in a heavy saucepan over a very low flame. Simmer gently until all the fat has been rendered and the chicken skin is very crisp and brown. Drain grebenes on paper towels and enjoy.

Chicken Burgers

2 cups leftover chicken (or turkey breast), ground
1 large onion, grated fine
2 large potatoes, raw, grated fine
2 eggs, well beaten
 flour seasoned with salt and pepper
 vegetable oil

After onion and potatoes are grated, drain for one hour in colander over sink, then mix with ground chicken (or turkey) and eggs. Form into 3"x4" patties; dip both sides in seasoned flour. Heat 1 tablespoon oil in large frying pan over medium heat; add patties and brown on both sides, adding more oil as needed. Makes 4 servings.

Baked Chicken with Rice

This recipe is perfect for a day when you're not going to have much time to prepare dinner. You can put it together in the morning, refrigerate it, and bake when you return home from work.

	rice (enough to cover the bottom of a 9"x13" casserole 1" deep)
1/2	cup cooking sherry
1/2	cup cooking sauterne
1/2	cup teriyaki sauce, bottled
1/2	cup water
12	chicken thighs
1/2	teaspoon dried minced onion
1/2	teaspoon dried minced garlic or garlic powder
	salt and pepper
1/4	teaspoon paprika
1/4	teaspoon oregano

Layer uncooked rice in the bottom of a greased casserole dish.
Place chicken pieces on top of rice.
Pour cooking sherry, sauterne and teriyaki sauce over chicken.
Sprinkle on spices to taste.
Cover the casserole with aluminum foil and punch a few holes in the foil.
Bake at 350° for 1-2 hours.
Makes 6-8 servings.

Spiced Chicken Livers

If you're tired of plain chopped liver, this recipe for Chinese-style chopped liver from our friend Lori McHugh is a good change.

1	pound chicken livers
1/2	cup each soy sauce and chopped green onions (including tops)
1/4	cup cooking sherry
1/2	teaspoon sugar
1/4	teaspoon anise seed
1 1/2	teaspoons chopped fresh ginger root OR 1 teaspoon ground ginger

Cover livers with water and bring just to boiling.
Remove from heat and drain well.
Return to heat and add soy sauce, green onions, sherry, sugar, anise seed and ginger.
Bring to boiling and simmer gently, covered, for 15 minutes.

Chill thoroughly in stock.
Slice livers into bite-sized pieces or process in food processor or blender until grainy.
Can be served cold or at room temperature; great with matzoh.
Makes 4-6 appetizer-size servings.

Nancy's Easy Chicken

At the Skokie Jews for Jesus potluck dinners, this dish is always a favorite.

  1   (3-pound) chicken, cut up (see Note)
  1   tablespoon oil (see Note)
  1   carrot, grated
  1   stalk celery, diced
  1   medium onion, diced
  1   (10½-ounce) can condensed cream of mushroom soup

Sauté chicken parts in oil in large frying pan over medium heat until lightly browned. Remove from pan; when cool, skin the chicken and cut into bite-sized pieces (this can be done in advance). In medium saucepan mix together cooked chicken and remaining ingredients. Bring to a boil over medium heat; lower heat and simmer, covered, 15 minutes or until vegetables are crisp-tender. Makes 4-6 servings.

Note: Nancy insists that this dish is best made with a kosher chicken, in which case no oil is needed for browning.

Cashew Chicken

This recipe received the Stuart Dauermann Stamp of Approval. Stuart's been known to eat anything, except radishes and beets. He's famous for the Jewish Gospel music he's written, and for his fondness for bananas. . .but that's another story.

  3   whole chicken breasts
  ½   pound snow peas OR 1 (10-ounce) package frozen snow peas
  ½   pound mushrooms
  1   (15-ounce) can bamboo shoots, drained
  1   cup chicken broth
  ¼   cup soy sauce
  4   green onions
  2   tablespoons cornstarch
  ½   teaspoon each sugar and salt
  ¼   cup oil or sesame oil
  ½   cup cashew nuts

Bone chicken breasts and remove skin. Slice into 1" squares. Remove ends from snow peas (or defrost frozen peas). Wash and slice mushrooms. Cut green onions into 1" lengths. Slice bamboo shoots (if not pre-sliced). Mix together soy sauce, cornstarch, sugar and salt. Heat 1 tablespoon oil to 350° (moderate heat) in wok or electric skillet; add nuts and cook 1 minute, until lightly toasted. Remove and set aside. Add remaining oil; add chicken and cook quickly, turning often until it turns opaque. Add peas, mushrooms and chicken broth, cover and simmer 2 minutes. Add bamboo shoots and green onion. Add soy sauce mixture and cook until sauce is thickened, stirring constantly. Add nuts. Serve over rice. Makes 4 servings.

Steve's Moroccan Chicken

Steve served on the Jews for Jesus missionary staff a number of years ago. He is a Jewish believer in Jesus who comes from a Moroccan background.

12	$^1/_2$-3 pound roasting or frying chicken, cut in pieces
$^1/_2$	teaspoon cinnamon
	salt, pepper
$^1/_2$	teaspoon ground turmeric
2	bay leaves
1	medium-sized onion
	vegetable oil
2-3	tablespoons honey
$^1/_2$	cup raisins

In a non-stick 2-quart pot, coat the bottom with a thin film of oil. Salt and pepper the chicken and cook over high heat until golden. Turn the heat to medium high and cover. Cook 20 minutes, adjusting the flame as necessary to keep the chicken from browning too much. Drain off most of the fat. Sprinkle the chicken with cinnamon and turmeric, rolling the chicken gently in the pot so it gets well coated with the spices. Add the bay leaves; cover and cook over medium heat for another 20 minutes (you'll have to stir the chicken a bit to keep it from sticking).

Meanwhile, chop the onion and sauté it in hot oil until it is lightly browned.

The chicken should now be getting tender. Add the sautéed onion, the honey and raisins. Cook slowly until the chicken is tender enough to melt in your mouth (about 5-15 minutes).
Makes 4 servings.

Turkey and Vegetable Lo Mein

Okay, so a turkey isn't a chicken. This recipe managed to find its way into this chapter anyway, and your family will devour it, we're sure. It is a good dish to bring to potlucks because it can be mixed in a large casserole, and is easily doubled. Chicken cutlets can be substituted for the turkey.

1	(16-ounce) package frozen mixed Oriental vegetables
4	cups cabbage, sliced
1 $^1/_4$	cups water
2	tablespoons soy sauce
1 $^1/_2$	tablespoons cornstarch
2	large cloves garlic, chopped
2	(3-ounce) packages Oriental beef-flavored ramen noodles
1	pound turkey cutlets (also called tenders or fillets), sliced crosswise into $^1/_8$" thick rounds OR
1	pound chicken cutlets, cut the same

Bring a large pot of water (3 quarts) to boil.

Place frozen vegetables and cabbage in boiling water, bring back to boil, lower heat and cook 10 minutes. Drain vegetables.

Mix together water, soy sauce, cornstarch, garlic and one of the seasoning packets from the ramen noodles. Place in a large pot and bring to a boil for one minute, stirring constantly until thickened.

Add turkey or chicken chunks; cook 4 minutes or until no longer pink.

Cook noodles according to package directions; drain.

Add noodles to vegetables, stirring all together.

Makes 4-6 servings.

Crockpot Chicken Cacciatori

Haul out your crockpot—you'll need it for this recipe. Although we're living in the day of the microwave, some recipes are still best suited for long, slow cooking in a crockpot. At one time crockpots were a standard kitchen item for most Jews for Jesus missionaries who worked such strange hours they were never sure when they'd get home to eat. Actually, our schedules haven't changed much, we just seem to rely more on microwave-ready foods these days. This chicken recipe is a throwback to the days of slow-simmered, delicious stews.

1	(28-ounce) can stewed tomatoes, mashed
1	(12-ounce) can tomato sauce
1	(6-ounce) can tomato paste
2	tomato paste cans of water
3	teaspoons Italian seasoning
2	teaspoons salt
	a shake or two of pepper
2	teaspoons garlic powder
	a pinch of rosemary and basil

Mix above ingredients together and simmer for 3 or 4 hours on low setting.

Then add:

1/2	pound mushrooms, sliced
1	large onion, chopped
1	green pepper, cut in strips

Simmer for 3 more hours on low.

Just before serving, add the meat of one cooked chicken, cut-up, and 3 tablespoons Parmesan cheese; cook until heated.

Makes 4-6 servings.

Indian Chicken with Sesame Seeds

Some recipes, like this one, sound more exotic than others.

1	(3-pound) frying chicken, cut up	2	tablespoons brown sugar
1/2	cup flour	2	tablespoons soy sauce
2	teaspoons salt	1/2	teaspoon ginger
1/2	teaspoon pepper	1	cup red wine
1	teaspoon paprika	1/3	cup toasted sesame seeds
3	tablespoons margarine or oil		

Place the first four ingredients (after the chicken) into a bag.
Shake chicken parts in bag.
Brown chicken lightly in butter in a heavy skillet and arrange in a baking pan.
To remaining fat in skillet add brown sugar, soy sauce, ginger and wine. Scrape up any remaining brown particles in the skillet; pour sauce over chicken in baking pan.
Toast seeds to a light golden brown and sprinkle over chicken.
Cover and bake 45-60 minutes at 350°.
Makes 4 servings.

Chopped Chicken Liver for a Jewish Wedding

Steve Wertheim often makes an enormous batch of his famous chopped liver for our Jews for Jesus wedding receptions. Because he realized that not everyone has the good fortune to attend these weddings, he's worked to scale down this recipe for home use. Chopped liver is good for any occasion, but especially when you're hungry.

5	pounds chicken livers
6	large onions
6	hard-boiled eggs
8-12	ounces chicken schmaltz or margarine (but schmaltz is better)

Wash livers and remove their membranes.
Meanwhile, heat some schmaltz in a skillet over low heat.
Chop the onions and fry in the schmaltz until very soft and light brown.
Add more schmaltz as needed and fry the livers in small batches only until lightly browned (if you overcook them they will be tough).
Transfer all to a wooden chopping bowl and chop until very fine.
When all the livers and onions are chopped, grate the hard-boiled eggs fine and mix in.
Add salt to taste and extra schmaltz if it needs more moistening.
Makes 16 appetizer-size servings.

Chicken and Spinach Pie

You can save time in making this recipe by using pre-roasted chicken, available in many supermarkets in the poultry section.

2   pounds assorted chicken pieces (your choice)
1   (8-ounce) jar chunky tomato sauce
1   (10-ounce) package frozen spinach, thawed
6   ounces mozzarella cheese, grated

Boil or roast chicken in your usual manner until bones slide out easily when pulled.
Remove skin from chicken.
Remove all bones, leaving chicken pieces as intact as you can.
Lay chicken pieces in the bottom of a greased baking pan.
Spread spinach in a layer over the chicken.
Cover with tomato sauce and grated cheese.
Cook in 350° oven until hot, or heat in microwave until cheese is melted and sauce is hot.
Makes 4 servings.

Continental Cornish Hens

We're not sure what continent this recipe is from, but it's delicious.

2   Cornish game hens, 1 $^1/_2$ pounds each
2   tablespoons softened butter or margarine
$^1/_2$ teaspoon tarragon
$^1/_4$ teaspoon salt
$^1/_8$ teaspoon garlic powder
$^1/_4$ cup chopped green onions
$^1/_3$ cup dry white wine or cooking wine

Rinse hens; pat dry; split in half; remove backbone.
Preheat oven to 400°.
Mix butter, tarragon, salt and garlic powder; spread over skin of hens.
Place hens skin-side up in 9"x13" baking pan.
Sprinkle green onions in dish, pour in wine.
Bake 30 minutes; baste; bake 30 minutes more. Skim fat off liquid.
Serve juices to spoon over hens.
Makes 2-4 servings.

Vegetables–Eat, They're Good for You!

Jewish people are famous for many things, but cooking vegetables hasn't been one of them. At family dinners, there are memorable meat dishes, soups, cakes and dairy dishes. I'm sure vegetables are there someplace, but they usually aren't especially noteworthy.

Perhaps this is due to the fact that, until recently, vegetables were probably the most misunderstood and poorly cooked of all foods. At one time, the only people who seemed even vaguely concerned about what to do with them was that odd bunch called vegetarians. They're the ones who started out drinking carrot juice and eating beet-top soup, but who ended up educating the rest of us about the necessity of eating vegetables. While most of us were marveling at the absence of meat in the vegetarians' shopping carts, they were becoming healthier and healthier. Today they have passed on their legacy of education about the vegetable, and now the entire country has become more vegetable-astute.
It is now impossible to treat the vegetable as anything less than a staple of a healthy diet. What could be more appetizing than a pan of slightly stewed tomatoes, bathed in a little olive oil and oregano, or a medley of vegetables topped with fresh Greek feta cheese. These recipes, and more, will be found in this chapter.

The current trend toward more healthful cooking has begun to make a slow impact on the Jewish cook. Bubbas of the future may still cook the life out of anything green, or may find themselves purchasing vegetable steamers along with other cooks. Perhaps we will even see such cookbooks as *From Bubba's Victory Garden* in the future. There's a slow, but definite movement, out of the garden and on to the table.

Lazy-Day Falafel

Lyn Rosen-Bond is one of Moishe and Ceil Rosen's daughters, the mother of Asher and Bethany, the wife of Oklahoma-born missionary Alan Bond and one of the un-laziest women I know. This recipe she offers is especially good for a day when you'd like to make something a little different but don't have a lot of time to spare.

Falafel is a typical Middle Eastern dish of mashed chickpeas and spices, which are rolled into little balls and deep fried. This recipe calls for the falafel to be baked instead of fried, thus saving time and calories. Lyn says, "If you are prone to heartburn, you might want to cut back on some of the spices. Otherwise, you might feel awful."

1	cup cooked, mashed potatoes
3	tablespoons dried parsley, chopped
3	cups cooked garbanzo beans (chickpeas), mashed or ground with course blade on food processor
1/4	cup sesame seed meal (run 1/4 cup sesame see through blender)
	juice of one lemon
3	cloves garlic, finely chopped
1/4	teaspoon salt
	dash black and cayenne pepper
1	teaspoon paprika
1	teaspoon ground turmeric
1/2	teaspoon cumin
1/2	teaspoon onion powder

Mix all ingredients together and form into balls, using 2 tablespoons mixture for each ball. Place on greased cookie sheet and bake for 10 minutes; turn, bake for 10 minutes more. Makes 8 servings.

Serve as is for appetizers or use to stuff into pita bread with yogurt or tehina dressing (see chapter on dips and dressings).

Spinach Quiche

What makes this quiche different is that the crust is made with Muenster cheese instead of flour.

12	ounces Muenster cheese, sliced	10	ounces ricotta cheese
3	(10-oz.) packages frozen, chopped spinach, defrosted and well drained	1/2	teaspoon salt
			pepper to taste
2	tablespoons dehydrated onion flakes		
2	eggs		

Line baking dish with half of the Muenster cheese. Mix remaining ingredients except Muenster and pour over as filling. Place remaining cheese slices over the top as a top crust. Bake at 375° for 30 minutes. Makes 6 servings.

Broccoli Mushroom Quiche

    1   cup fresh mushrooms, sliced
    2   cups cooked, chopped broccoli
    2   cups grated Swiss cheese
  1/3   cup minced onion
        unbaked 9" pie shell
    4   eggs
    2   cups half and half
  3/4   teaspoon salt
  1/4   teaspoon sugar
  1/8   teaspoon cayenne pepper
        cooking oil

Sauté sliced mushrooms in small amount of oil until lightly cooked. Place a layer of cooked broccoli, then sautéed mushrooms, then grated Swiss cheese and minced onion in the pie shell. Mix together eggs, cream, salt, sugar and cayenne pepper in bowl; pour over layered vegetables and cheese. Bake at 425° for 15 minutes; lower oven to 300° and bake 30 minutes more. Test to see if knife comes out clean. Let quiche stand 10 minutes before cutting. Makes 6 servings.

Serbian Spinach

    1   (10-ounce) package frozen   1/4-1/2   pound cheddar cheese, cubed
        chopped spinach,   3   eggs, slightly beaten
        defrosted and drained   1   teaspoon salt
    1   pound small curd cottage cheese   3   tablespoons flour
    4   tablespoons butter or
        margarine, cut in cubes

Mix all ingredients thoroughly in large bowl. Spread in 2-quart greased baking dish. Bake at 350° for 45-50 minutes (the cheese cubes near the top will look browned). Makes 4 servings.

Chickpea Curry ala Landrum

Rahel Landrum is an Israeli believer who serves as a missionary in our Chicago branch.
    1   (16-ounce) can chickpeas (also called garbanzo beans)
    2   tablespoons cooking oil
    1   medium onion, chopped
    2   cloves garlic, chopped
    2   canned green chilies
    1   teaspoon salt
  1/2   teaspoon pepper
    1   coriander leaf
    1   mint leaf

1   teaspoon ground cumin
1   teaspoon ground turmeric
4   cloves
4   cardamom pods
2   tablespoons tomato puree

Drain the chickpeas. Sauté the onion and garlic in 2 tablespoons oil in a saucepan until soft.
Add all the spices and cook for 2 minutes, stirring constantly.
Add the chickpeas and 1 cup water.
Bring to a boil and simmer for 15 minutes, covered, or until the chickpeas are soft.
Stir in the tomato puree and cook for 1 minute more.
Remove cloves and cardamon pods before serving.
Makes 4 servings.

Greek Vegetable Skillet

$^1/_3$ cup olive oil
$^1/_2$ pound zucchini, cut into
      $^3/_4$" slices
1 $^1/_2$ pounds eggplant, cubed
$^1/_2$ cup onion, chopped
1   (16-ounce) can tomatoes
2   teaspoons dried mint

2   teaspoons dried dillweed
$^1/_2$ teaspoon salt
$^1/_2$ teaspoon pepper
$^1/_2$ cup plain yogurt
$^3/_4$ pound feta cheese, crumbled

Heat oil in large skillet. Sauté first three vegetables for 5 minutes, stirring constantly.
Add tomatoes (undrained), mint, dillweed, salt and pepper.
Cover and cook 15 minutes over low heat. Stir in yogurt and heat for 3 minutes.
Before serving, crumble feta cheese over the top.
Makes 4-6 servings.

Carrot Squash Boats

2   acorn squash, about 1 pound each
6   carrots
2   teaspoons sugar
1   teaspoon salt
2   tablespoons butter

Halve squash and remove seeds. Place cut side down in baking dish.
Pour in hot water up to $^1/_2$". Bake 30 minutes at 400°.
Pare and shred carrots; stir in sugar, salt and pepper.
Remove squash from oven, fill cavities with carrot mixture and dot with butter.
Bake 30 minutes more.
Makes 4 servings.

Lowfat Baked Zucchini Casserole

2	pounds zucchini, grated
1	large onion, grated
	cholesterol-and-fat-free egg substitute to equal 4 eggs
1/4	cup parsley, chopped or 2 tablespoons dried parsley flakes
1/2	teaspoon dried dillweed
1/3	cup flour
2	tablespoons olive oil
1/2	teaspoon salt
1/4	teaspoon pepper

Place grated zucchini and onion in a colander over sink to drain. In large bowl, mix together grated vegetables, egg substitute, spices, flour and 1 tablespoon of the oil. Heat remaining tablespoon oil in 8"x8" casserole in oven set at 375°. Add vegetable mixture. Bake until set, about 50-60 minutes. Makes 8 servings.

Mrs. Lougheed's Savory Spinach

We're not sure who Mrs. Lougheed is.

Combine and mix:

2/3	cup milk	2	teaspoons salt
1/4	cup melted butter	1/2	tablespoon dried thyme
1/2	cup onion, minced	1/2	tablespoon nutmeg
2	tablespoons dry parsley flakes	4	eggs, beaten
1	tablespoon Worcestershire sauce		

Add:
2 (10-ounce) packages frozen chopped spinach, cooked and drained
2 cups cooked rice
2 cups grated cheddar cheese

Bake at 350° for 40-45 minutes. Makes 6 servings.

Spinach Latkes (Croquetas de Espinaca)

This is one of Zhava Glaser's authentic Argentine recipes.

2	eggs
1/2	cup milk
1 1/2	cups flour
2	tablespoons Parmesan cheese

1   (16-ounce) can spinach, drained or 2 (10-ounce) packages chopped frozen spinach,
    cooked and well drained
    vegetable oil
1   cup bread crumbs (or more as needed)

Beat eggs with milk, add flour and Parmesan cheese and mix well. Add spinach. Form into latkes (or croquettes), coat with bread crumbs and fry in small amount of oil in frying pan. Add more flour if latkes won't hold their shape.

Variations: you can also add cooked corn kernels or pieces of chopped frankfurters to the spinach latkes.

Sauerkraut to Convince You

From the loquacious Lois Link, who wore many hats and aprons at our San Francisco office, comes this unique way of cooking kraut. She says that she never did like sauerkraut until she tasted it made this way.

1   quart sauerkraut (rinsed to lower the salt content, if desired)
1   cup water
1/4 cup sugar (or more, to taste)

Combine and cook over very low heat for 15 minutes.
2   tablespoons margarine
2   tablespoons flour

Melt margarine in small pan until very hot. Add flour and stir until browned. Add to kraut and heat until slightly thickened. Makes 4-6 servings.

Copper Pennies

3   pounds carrots, sliced
1   small green pepper, thinly sliced
1   medium onion, thinly sliced
1   (10 1/2-ounce) can condensed tomato soup (do not dilute)
1/2 cup vegetable oil
1/2 cup sugar
3/4 cup vinegar
1   teaspoon prepared mustard
1   teaspoon Worcestershire sauce
    salt

Cook carrots in small amount of water until done, drain. Arrange carrots, green pepper and onion in a glass dish or other suitable container. Combine remaining ingredients in a saucepan, bring to a boil, stir. Pour marinade over vegetable mixture and refrigerate 24 hours. Can be served hot or cold. This will keep a few weeks in the refrigerator. Makes 8 servings.

Lyonnaise Carrots

1   (20-ounce) package frozen carrots, cooked
1   medium onion, sautéed in 1 tablespoon margarine or butter

Mix together in casserole and bake at 350° until vegetables are lightly browned (about 10-15 minutes). Makes 6 servings.

Baked Asparagus with Pine Nuts

1   teaspoon margarine
1   pound asparagus, cleaned, tough ends snapped off
$1/2$ cup Gruyere or Parmesan cheese, grated
3   tablespoons pine nuts
1   tablespoon olive oil

Melt margarine in large, ovenproof skillet (with cover). In same skillet, line up asparagus with tips facing in one direction. Add 3 tablespoons water and cover. Steam for 2 minutes over medium heat. Remove from heat and sprinkle cheese over top. Strew pine nuts over the cheese and dribble with olive oil. Bake, uncovered, at 350° for 5 minutes. Makes 4 servings.

Sautéed Bean Sprouts

2   cups fresh bean sprouts
1   tablespoon vegetable oil
$1/2$ teaspoon salt
1   large yellow squash, halved lengthwise, seeded and shredded
1   medium carrot, peeled and shredded
2   green onions, trimmed, cut into 2-inch pieces and sliced lengthwise
1   tablespoon cooking sherry

In large skillet, heat oil over high heat. Sauté sprouts for 1 minute. Sprinkle with $1/4$ teaspoon of the salt. Add squash, carrot and green onions; sauté until the carrots are tender, about 2 minutes. Stir in remaining salt. Remove from heat. Add sherry. Makes 4 servings.

Hot Spiced Beets

If you like beets, you'll love these. If you're lukewarm about beets, you'll love these. If you don't like beets, skip this recipe!

1   (16-ounce) can sliced beets, drained (reserve liquid)

$^1/_4$	teaspoon ground cloves
$^1/_2$	teaspoon salt
$^1/_8$	teaspoon cinnamon
2	tablespoons brown sugar
1	tablespoon white sugar
$^1/_8$	cup white or apple cider vinegar

Place beets in medium saucepan. In small saucepan heat together remaining ingredients. Pour over beets and heat over low flame. Makes 4 servings.

Vegetable Casserole

1	(20-ounce) bag mixed frozen vegetables, cooked until done, drained
$^1/_2$	pound processed cheese spread, cubed
2-4	slices of white bread, cubed
1	($10^1/_2$-ounce) can condensed cream of mushroom soup
1	stick margarine, melted

Mix all ingredients together in medium, greased casserole dish. Bake 350° for 40-45 minutes. Makes 4-6 servings.

A Vegetable Dish for Non-Cooks

This recipe was submitted by Jo Ann Farris, who admits she's sometimes too lazy to measure her ingredients.

"Take a bunch of veggies, like broccoli, cauliflower, carrots, zucchini and fresh mushrooms. Cut them into large pieces (but individual portions). Boil the veggies (I boil them because I'm too lazy to be healthy and steam them, and if you boil them they cook faster—and besides, I like mushy vegetables). Take 2 to 4 cans cheddar cheese soup, without diluting them, and heat them up in a saucepan. Drain the veggies and mix with the soup. Shred a whole lot of cheddar cheese, or whatever you have on hand. Put the vegetable/cheese soup mixture in a nice-looking casserole. Top with the shredded cheese, some grated Parmesan cheese and bacon bits (from a jar). Heat on HIGH in microwave until hot and cheese is slightly melted, about three minutes. Everyone will think you slaved for hours coming up with this. But be careful not to overcook the veggies. It begins to look like soup if you do."

Another Farris Vegtable Dish

"Open 2-3 1-pound cans of green beans. Drain. Open 2-3 cans of cream of mushroom soup. Heat the soup. Put the green beans into a nice-looking casserole dish. Pour the soup over top and mix beans and soup together. Shred a whole lot of cheddar cheese. Top casserole with cheddar, grated Parmesan cheese and bacon bits. Place in microwave on HIGH for 2-3 minutes. Everyone will ask for your recipe!"

Karen's Pumpkin Au Gratin

Karen Breen is a Jewish believer who was raised in New Jersey but found her way to Chicago. She has beautiful red hair, is a wonderful cook and a good friend of the Moskowitz's, who have lost count of how many cups of coffee they've consumed at Karen's house. This unusual recipe is time-consuming to make, but Karen selflessly prepares it for us whenever we ask (well, not every time, but enough to warrant putting it in this cookbook).

2	pound piece pumpkin (or other hard squash, such as butternut or acorn)
	flour seasoned with salt and pepper
	vegetable oil
1	pound onions, sliced
1	(16-ounce) can tomatoes, drained
	salt and pepper, sugar
$1/4$-$1/2$	cup bread crumbs
2	tablespoons butter or margarine

Peel the pumpkin or squash, remove the seeds and cut into $1/4$" thick by 2" wide slices. Turn the pieces in seasoned flour and fry in hot oil until golden but not brown. Cook one layer at a time, draining pieces on paper towels as they are finished. In another pan, cook the onions in a few tablespoons of oil until they are soft but not colored. Add tomatoes and simmer until well-moistened. Season with salt and pepper and a little sugar. In a greased casserole, layer pumpkin with onions, adding a little salt and pepper and ending with pumpkin. Scatter with bread crumbs. Melt butter or margarine and drizzle over all. Bake at 350° for 45 minutes. Makes 6-8 servings.

Donna's Mock Pesto with Vegetables

Some artists are cooks, some cooks are artists. Donna Byrne is both. She lives in Evanston, Illinois with her husband Richard and two beautiful daughters, Tali and Tamar. The Byrnes own the Great Lakes Foundry, a company that casts and creates bronze sculptures. When Donna is not busy creating her own sculptures, she can be found in her kitchen inventing new recipes for the vegetables she and her husband grow each year.

6-7	sundried tomatoes
	about 5 tablespoons olive oil
3	large cloves garlic, minced
1	medium eggplant (see Variation)
1	medium green pepper, cut into $1/4$" strips
1	medium red pepper, cut into $1/4$" strips
	about 1 $1/2$ cups chicken broth, heated to boiling
2	tablespoons basil puree (see Note)
3-4	tablespoons freshly grated Parmesan cheese
$1/3$	cup coarsely chopped walnuts

Put sundried tomatoes in bowl and cover with water; set aside. Quarter eggplant and cut into $1/4$" slices. In large frying pan with cover, heat 3 tablespoons olive oil over medium heat. Add garlic and cook until softened, but not brown. Add eggplant slices and sauté, stirring, for about ten minutes or until softened. Add green and red peppers to pan, adding more oil as needed. Cook over medium heat about 10 minutes. Drain water from tomatoes; dice. Add tomatoes to pan, along with 1 $1/4$ cups chicken broth. Cover and cook over low heat until all vegetables are softened, adding more broth if vegetables seem too dry. Add basil puree and Parmesan cheese, mixing well. Serve over fettucine or linguine, cooked al dente. Sprinkle chopped walnuts over all. Makes 4-6 servings.

Variation: 1 pound asparagus, with tough ends snapped off, cut into 1" pieces, can be substituted for eggplant. Also, cooked strips of chicken or veal cutlet, or turkey or veal sausage cut into $1/4$" rounds and cooked until browned, can be mixed into dish when cooked.

Note: To make basil puree, take seven cups washed fresh basil leaves and blend or process with three tablespoons olive oil. Keep refrigerated or frozen and use as needed.

Zucchini Casserole

Faithfulness is a gift of the spirit, and Delores Howard is blessed with it. Her recipe won first prize in a local synagogue cooking contest.

2	tablespoons butter or margarine
$1/4$	onion, chopped
1	clove garlic, crushed
2	pounds zucchini, cut into $1/2$" chunks
$1/2$	teaspoon salt
	pinch pepper
16	cherry tomatoes, cut in half
4	ounces Cheddar cheese, cubed
$1/2$	cup soft breadcrumbs
2	tablespoons butter or margarine, melted

Heat butter or margarine in frying pan. Sauté onion and garlic until tender. Add zucchini, salt and pepper; cook for 5 minutes. Layer zucchini mixture alternately with tomatoes and cheese in greased 1 $1/2$ quart casserole. Combine crumbs with melted butter and sprinkle on top of casserole. Bake at 350° for 25 minutes. Makes 6-8 servings.

Spinach with Garlic

2	tablespoons olive oil
1	clove garlic, crushed
1	(10-ounce) package frozen chopped spinach
$1/2$	teaspoon salt

Brown garlic lightly in olive oil in small saucepan; remove from pan. Add frozen spinach and salt; cover. Cook over low heat until spinach is heated through. Makes 3-4 servings.

The Moskowitz Children's Spinach

Kayla and Jessie discovered spinach later in life (ages 8 and 12, respectively). This dish was created for them when there were no other vegetables in the refrigerator for dinner. Surprisingly, the children ate all the spinach.

1	(10-ounce) package frozen chopped spinach
1/4	pound feta cheese, crumbled
1/2	teaspoon oregano

Cook spinach in microwave according to package directions (or in small saucepan over low heat—no additional water is necessary). Stir in crumbled feta and oregano; return to heat until feta begins to melt slightly. Makes 3-4 servings.

Squash Delight

Cecilia Butcher offers us this easy, but delicious recipe that she says is a favorite at church potlucks.

3	cups sliced zucchini
1	(10 1/2-ounce) can condensed cream of mushroom soup
1	cup sour cream
1	cup onion, chopped
1/2	cup seasoned stuffing mix
1/2	cup Parmesan cheese, grated

Cook or steam zucchini in small amount of salted water until done. Mix next three ingredients together in medium bowl. Make layers of zucchini and soup mixture in greased casserole. Top all with seasoned stuffing mix and Parmesan cheese. Bake at 350° for 25 minutes, or until heated through. Makes 4-6 servings.

Vegetable Pizza

1	(8-ounce) package refrigerated crescent rolls
8	ounces cream cheese, softened
1	teaspoon garlic powder
1/3	cup mayonnaise
1	teaspoon packaged dry Italian salad dressing mix
	few drops olive oil
1-2	cups leftover cooked vegetables
	Parmesan cheese, grated

Unwrap crescent rolls and press into 9"x13" pan. Bake 11-13 minutes at 350°. Cool. Mix remaining ingredients together with electric beater. Spread over cooled crust. Cover with leftover cooked vegetables (broccoli, red pepper, sliced tomatoes, cauliflower). Sprinkle several tablespoons grated Parmesan cheese over top. Bake for 25 minutes or until hot. Makes 6 servings.

. . .And Side Dishes, Just in Case You're Still Hungry

This cookbook needed a chapter called "And" (although some may think that it needs it like a hole in the head!). Where else would we put our recipes for all those other dishes— potatoes, rice, noodles and beans—that round out a meal? In a Jewish home, it's not enough to have just a good meal; you have to leave the table stuffed in order to please the Jewish mama who served you. Now, we're not advocating gluttony, but if you want an authentic Jews for Jesus dining experience, you must add at least one of these dishes to your menu.

But side dishes are not a uniquely Jewish invention. Many of the recipes in this chapter are from some expert non-Jewish cooks, too. In fact, some of the best contributions came from our Co-Laborers in Messiah program. This program was designed to give Gentiles who love the Jewish people a chance to volunteer with Jews for Jesus. Headed up by Cecilia Butcher, the Co-Laborers program is one of the unseen backbones of the Jews for Jesus ministry, reaching out in areas of the country where we do not have branch offices. Some of our Co-Laborers are so busy working for the Lord, we do not know when they find time to cook, but cook they do, and quite well indeed.

This chapter is divided into three sections: 1) dairy and eggs, 2) potatoes, 3) rice and beans. There's a little bit of this, and a little bit of that. A few of the dishes are substantial enough to make a meal by themselves when served with a green salad or vegetable. Some are traditional Jewish dishes, while others hail from the far corners of this country.

Section One–Dairy and Eggs

Joyful Eggs Estrada

When you're part of a Jews for Jesus mobile evangelistic team, you're afforded many unique opportunities. You meet more than your average share of people, rest overnight in more than your average share of homes and eat more than your average share of terrific food. The McMillans of Detroit are two of those above-average people our teams have met on the road. Whenever we've stayed at their home, Joy makes her famous Eggs Estrada for breakfast. Joy's name aptly describes her, as she bubbles over with the joy of the Lord.

16	slices bread (preferably white)—crusts removed
2	cups turkey ham, in strips or diced
8-10	ounces cheddar cheese, grated
6	eggs
$1/2$	teaspoon salt
3	cups milk
$1/2$	teaspoon dry mustard
1	cup crushed cornflakes
$1/4$	cup melted butter or margarine
	extra butter or margarine

Butter 8 slices of bread; arrange butter-side down in a 11"x7" baking dish. Top with ham and grated cheese. Place remaining 8 slices of bread on top. Mix milk, eggs, salt and mustard together in a large bowl; pour over the sandwiches. Cover dish with plastic wrap and refrigerate overnight. Before baking, uncover dish and top sandwiches with crushed cornflakes and drizzle $1/4$ cup melted butter or margarine over all. Bake, uncovered, for 1 hour at 350°. Makes 6-8 servings.

Aunt Maxine's Pineapple Cheese Casserole

1	(20-ounce) can chunk pineapple in its own juice, well drained (reserve juice)
$1/4$	cup sugar
$1/8$	cup flour
1	cup cheddar cheese, grated

Place pineapple in shallow, greased baking dish.
Mix together sugar and flour, and sprinkle over top.
Gently pour in reserved pineapple juice.
Sprinkle cheese over all.
Bake, uncovered, 30 minutes at 350°.
Makes 4 servings.

Grandma Broom's Homemade Noodles

Who makes homemade noodles these days? Sue Rothberg's Grandma Broom still makes her own noodles. Sue says, "Whenever our family would visit at Grandma's house, she would have a big kettle of freshly made noodles waiting for us. This recipe has been on my mother's side of the family for generations, and are my grandmother's specialty. Whenever I make them I'm reminded of the warm, special times we had together as a family at her home." Our thanks to Grandma Broom. Perhaps these noodles will help you make some memories of your own.

      4   cups whole wheat flour
               OR
      3   cups white flour (whichever you prefer)
      3   eggs
      1   teaspoon salt
      2   tablespoons water

Place flour in large mixing bowl, and make well in center of flour. Place eggs in well and gradually stir the flour into eggs. Add salt and water and knead dough in bowl. Turn dough out onto floured board, knead well, and roll thin into a 16"-18" circle. Let dry until tough, then cut into thin strips (you can cut the dough into $1/4$'s, then $1/8$'s, and so on). Bring a large pot of water (or beef or chicken broth) to a boil and gradually add the noodles, stirring constantly. Cover and cook over low heat for 30 minutes (whole wheat noodles may take a little longer). Makes 6-8 servings.

Blintzes, of Course

This cookbook would not be complete if we didn't offer a recipe for blintzes. These are the Jewish egg roll plus. Blintzes are to Jewish homes what tacos are to Mexicans, a staple of life. This recipe for blintzes comes from Ellen Zaretsky's mother. Blintzes can be fattening, but Ellen's skinny husband Tuvya, and their three beautiful children don't seem to mind.

Blintze wrappers:
      4   eggs, beaten
      1   cup milk
      1   cup flour
      1   teaspoon salt

Combine beaten eggs with milk and salt. Gradually add this mixture to flour. Beat until smooth. Heat a heavy 6" skillet and grease lightly with butter or margarine. Pour in only enough batter to make a very thin pancake, tilting pan from side to side to cover bottom. Fry on one side only, until blintze blisters. Turn out onto floured waxed paper, fried side up. Repeat until all batter is used.

Cheese filling:
      1   pound dry curd cottage cheese
      2   tablespoons flour
      2   tablespoons sugar
      1   teaspoon ground cinnamon

Mix together cheese, flour, sugar and cinnamon. Place a well-rounded tablespoon of mixture in center of blintze wrapper. Fold over both sides toward center and roll into envelope shape. Blintzes may be frozen at this point and browned in 350° oven when ready to serve. Fry blintzes in butter or margarine on both sides until brown. Handle gently. Serve with sour cream or jelly. Makes 6 servings.

Blintze Casserole

This recipe for blintze casserole is one of our favorites, as it by-passes the process of making the individual blintze wrappers called for in traditional recipes.

Batter:
- 1 cup butter, melted
- 3 eggs
- 1/4 cup milk
- 1 teaspoon vanilla
- 1 cup flour
- 1/2 cup sugar
- 3 teaspoons baking powder
- dash salt

Filling:
- 2 pounds small curd cottage cheese
- 3 eggs
- 1/4 cup sugar
- juice of 1 lemon

Mix all batter ingredients together. Mix all filling ingredients together in separate bowl. To assemble casserole: Preheat oven to 300°. Grease bottom of 2-quart baking dish. Place half of batter in baking dish. Pour in all the filling. Top with remaining batter. Bake 1 1/2 hours and serve with sour cream or jelly. Makes 8 servings.

Ask My Mother-in-Law Blintzes

When I was a new bride of two weeks, I decided to surprise my husband Jhan by making cheese blintzes, for surely this would establish my ability as a Jewish wife. When I set a dish of beautifully browned blintzes before my husband, he made the one fatal mistake that a Jewish (or even non-Jewish) husband can make. After taking a few bites he remarked, "They're good, but they're not like my mother's."

I never made blintzes again.

Four years later, after the birth of our first child, Jhan's mother came to see her new grandchild. The morning after the proud grandma had arrived, Jhan marched us both into the kitchen and said, "Today my mother is going to teach you how to make blintzes." Out came the frying pans. Out came the flour, the measuring spoons and the spatula. Out came the pad of paper and pencil with which I planned to write down every step of my mother-in-law's preparations. At first, the process went along quite well. But when Jhan's mother pushed aside the measuring cups and added a handful more of flour and a soup spoon more of milk, I pushed aside the pad and pencil, poured myself a cup of coffee, and watched the preparations from the safe distance of the kitchen table. No longer the eager learner, I resigned myself to the position of eager eater, and enjoyed several blintzes.

To this day our family rarely has homemade blintzes in our home, but I do encourage Jhan and the children to eat them at restaurants and in my mother-in-law's kitchen.

Forman's Formidable Buckwheat Blinis with Caviar

This recipe is a testimony to the fact that if you bother somebody long enough, they'll give you what you want just to get rid of you! Mitch Forman has a reputation as a professional chef, and it was agreed that he had to live up to his image and contribute something to this cookbook. However, like all Jews for Jesus, Mitch has been very busy wearing several different hats besides his chef's—and now he's a full-time missionary with even less free time to devote to cooking. There are several original Forman recipes in this cookbook, which we are proud to reveal to all of you.

$^1/_2$	ounce yeast
$^1/_2$	cup warm water
8	ounces flour
8	ounces buckwheat flour
2	egg yolks
2	egg whites
1	tablespoon heavy cream
16	ounces smoked salmon
$^1/_2$	cup sour cream
1	ounce black or red caviar

Dissolve the yeast in the warm water.
Combine yeast with the next four ingredients.
Add the whites.
Let the mixture stand in the refrigerator for 1 hour.
Heat a griddle to 375° degrees; spray with vegetable shortening.
Pour out 2 ounces of batter and cook like a pancake.
Cook on one side until golden brown (1 minute), turn over and finish cooking (2 minutes).
On a dinner plate take 4 ounces of the smoked salmon and cover the bottom of the plate.
Place 3 blinis in the center of the plate and top each blini with a teaspoon of sour cream and a teaspoon of caviar.
Makes 16 blinis to serve 4 people.

McHugh's Noodle Kugel (Pudding)

What's a nice Jewish girl like Lori doing with a name like McHugh? Lori's a Jewish believer married to an Irish believer, Tom, and they both served in the Liberated Wailing Wall mobile evangelistic music team for several years. Now that she's been living in one place—Connecticut—she has lots of time to cook. Lori writes about the following recipe: "A distinct advantage of being one of the few Jewish believers in our church is that I know no one else will bring a noodle kugel to our potluck dinners." Although there are many ways to cook kugel, this one is guaranteed to be a hit, especially with the Irish.

1	(16-ounce) package broad egg noodles
6	eggs
1	cup sugar
2	cups (16-ounces) sour cream
2	cups (16-ounces) cottage cheese
1 1/2	cups milk
1	cup raisins
4	tablespoons butter, melted
2	teaspoons vanilla extract
	cinnamon (optional)

Cook noodles according to package directions; drain. In large bowl, beat eggs and sugar together, blend in milk, sour cream, cottage cheese, raisins, butter and vanilla. Add noodles and toss gently to blend well. Turn into 4-quart baking dish, greased, and sprinkle with cinnamon, if desired. Bake 1 hour at 350° or until golden. Serve hot or cold, topped with additional sour cream if desired. Makes 10-12 servings.

Momma's Noodle Pudding

Janie-sue Wertheim has graced our ears with the music she's written and sung for the Jews for Jesus ministry. Those of us who know her well also know she's a great cook. This recipe for noodle kugel was handed down from her mother. What distinguishes it from other noodle kugels is the addition of crushed pineapple (or applesauce, if you prefer).

1	(16-ounce) package broad egg noodles
2	cups (16 ounces) cottage cheese
1	pint sour cream
1	cup raisins
3	eggs, well beaten
1	stick (1/2 cup) butter or margarine
6	tablespoons brown sugar
1	teaspoon cinnamon
1	cup crushed, drained pineapple (or 1 cup applesauce)

Cook noodles according to package directions; drain well. Use half of the stick of butter or margarine to grease a 13"x9" baking dish; melt the other half and add to the noodles in a large mixing bowl. Add all other ingredients and mix together well. Bake for 45 minutes at 375° or until top is golden brown. Makes 12-16 servings.

Shredded Apple Noodle Kugel

1/2   pound broad egg noodles
3   eggs, beaten
1   pound cottage cheese
4   tablespoons sour cream
1/4   pound butter or margarine
3   apples, shredded with skins on
1/2   cup raisins
1   teaspoon salt
1/4   cup sugar
1   teaspoon cinnamon

Prepare noodles according to package directions; drain well.
Mix together in bowl with remaining ingredients.
Place in greased 11"x7" baking dish.
Bake for 1 hour at 350° or until golden brown.
Serve warm or cold with sour cream.
Makes 6 servings

Another Noodle Pudding

1/2   pound noodles, broad or fine
2   eggs, beaten
3   tablespoons sugar
1/4   teaspoon cinnamon
4   tablespoons butter, melted
1/2   cup raisins
   pinch salt

Cook noodles according to package directions; drain well.
Combine all ingredients and mix well.
Place in a well-buttered 1 1/2 quart casserole and bake at 400° approximately 45 minutes, or until brown.
Makes 6 servings.

Optional: 1/4 cup chopped walnuts or pecans and 1 cup shredded tart apple can be added.

Okay, Just One More Noodle Kugel

$^1/_2$ pound broad noodles, cooked
1 $^1/_4$ pounds apples, sliced thin (you can leave peels on)
2   tablespoons butter or margarine
1   cup raisins
1 $^1/_4$ cups milk
5   eggs
$^1/_2$ tablespoon cinnamon
$^1/_4$ cup sugar
    cinnamon/sugar for sprinkling
    butter or margarine to dot on top

Combine all ingredients together, mixing well. Pour into greased 7"x11" or 9"x13" baking pan; sprinkle top with cinnamon/sugar and dot with butter or margarine. Bake at 325° about 35 minutes, or until browned on top. Makes 6-8 servings

Baked Noodles with Spinach and Yogurt

4   ounces broad egg noodles
1   (8-ounce) container plain yogurt
$^1/_2$ cup cottage cheese
1   (10-ounce) package frozen chopped spinach, thawed
2   tablespoons onion, chopped
$^1/_2$ cup cheddar cheese, shredded

Cook noodles according to package directions; drain. Combine yogurt and cottage cheese in 1-quart baking dish. Add noodles, thawed spinach, onions and cottage cheese mixture. Top with cheddar cheese. Cover and bake at 400° for 20-25 minutes. Uncover and bake until cheese is melted and browned. Makes 2-3 servings, but can easily be doubled or tripled.

A Slightly Different Spinach-Cheese-and-Noodle Dish

8   ounces medium or wide egg noodles, uncooked
1   tablespoon oil
1   large clove garlic, minced
1   (10-ounce) package frozen chopped spinach, thawed and drained
2   teaspoons fresh minced basil OR $^1/_2$ teaspoon dried basil
$^1/_4$ cup minced fresh parsley OR 1 tablespoon dried parsley
1   cup lowfat cottage cheese
$^1/_4$ teaspoon salt
2   tablespoons grated Parmesan cheese

Cook noodles according to package directions. Drain and keep warm. Meanwhile, heat oil in 10" frying pan and sauté the garlic and spinach, stirring for 5 minutes. Add basil, parsley, cottage cheese, salt and pepper. Cook the mixture over very low heat, stirring until it is well blended and heated through, about 2 minutes. Add spinach and cheese mixture to the cooked noodles; toss to combine. Sprinkle with Parmesan cheese and serve. Makes 4-6 servings.

Sesame Noodles

Do not serve this dish to Jhan Moskowitz, as he is violently allergic to sesame oil.

$1/4$	cup creamy peanut butter
1	tablespoon honey
2	teaspoons vinegar
1	tablespoon soy sauce
$1/4$-$1/2$	cup chicken broth or bouillon
$1/2$	teaspoon sesame oil
$1/4$	teaspoon tabasco
$1/2$-1	pound cooked soba noodles (or thin spaghetti)
	green onions, cucumber—julienned for garnish

Mix all ingredients except noodles and garnish in small bowl until well mixed (can be whirled in blender). Pour over cooked noodles to coat strands evenly. Garnish with julienned vegetables. Makes 4-8 servings, depending upon how much noodles you use.

Kreplach (Noodle Turnovers Filled with Meat)

Dough:

1	egg, slightly beaten
$1/4$	teaspoon salt
1	cup flour, sifted

Filling:

2	tablespoons onion, minced
2	tablespoons margarine
1	egg
1	cup cooked ground beef
$1/2$	teaspoon salt

Make dough of egg, salt and flour by beating well together with wooden spoon. Knead on floured board until elastic. Roll paper-thin; cut into 2"-3" squares. Mix remaining ingredients for filling; place heaping teaspoonful on half of each square. Fold remaining half over top to make triangles. Press edges together securely. Drop into large pot of boiling salted water, cover tightly and cook for 20 minutes. Makes 6 servings.

Toasted Cheese Ravioli

- 1   tablespoon olive oil
- 1   (9 ounce) package fresh cheese ravioli, cooked, rinsed, tossed in a little oil, chilled
- 1/2   cup red onion, chopped fine
- 1   (14 1/2-ounce) can plum tomatoes, undrained
- 2   tablespoons balsamic vinegar
- 1/4   teaspoon salt
- 1/3   cup fresh basil, chopped (or 1 tablespoon dried basil)
     grated Parmesan

Heat oil in large skillet over high heat. Add ravioli, making sure to separate any that stick together. Toast on both sides until crisp-tender, about four minutes. Remove from pan and set aside. Add onions to pan (with a little water if necessary, to keep from sticking). Stir-fry until heated, about 2 minutes. Add tomatoes and their liquid, vinegar and salt. Bring to a boil for about 2 minutes. Add ravioli; stir-fry 30 seconds. Add basil. Toss well and serve with grated Parmesan. Makes 4 servings.

Section Two—Potatoes

Nanna's Potato Kugel

When Loren Jacobs was growing up, Nanna's potato kugel was his favorite food. Now that he's grown up, he admits that it's still his favorite food! His grandmother makes it especially for him whenever he visits her. She sits there and kvells (beams with pride and delight) while he eats the entire kugel. Now, not all of the Jews for Jesus are so fortunate to be as skinny as Loren, so we're all a little envious. Limit yourself to just a small piece when you make this kugel.

    4   large potatoes, peeled
    1   onion
    2   eggs
        chicken fat (schmaltz)—not butter or margarine
        salt and pepper
        paprika

Grate potatoes and onions together in food processor. Mix in eggs and season to taste liberally with salt and pepper. Grease a 9-inch pie pan liberally with chicken fat and fold mixture into pan. Dot top with small bits of chicken fat and sprinkle lightly with paprika. Bake at 350° until top is lightly brown, about 45 minutes. Serves 1 Loren Jacobs or 4 regular people.

Potato Pancakes (Latkes)

    1/4   cup milk
      2   eggs
      3   cups raw, diced potatoes
      1   small onion, quartered
      3   tablespoons flour
      1   teaspoon salt
    1/4   teaspoon baking powder
          oil

Put all ingredients (except oil) in food processor in order indicated and process until well-blended, but not overprocessed.
Heat oil to cover bottom of large frying pan to 1/4".
Drop in heaping tablespoons of potato mixture (use about 1/4 cup mixture per pancake).
Fry on one side until golden brown; turn and brown other side.
Drain on paper towels.
Makes 1 dozen.

Oven-Baked French Fries

1 ½   pounds large russet or other baking potatoes
1   teaspoon chili powder
2   teaspoons oil
¼   teaspoon salt

Put a large baking sheet in the oven and preheat the oven to 475°.
Cut potatoes lengthwise into slices about ½" thick.
Cut each slice lengthwise into ½" thick strips and place them in a large bowl.
Toss the potato strips with chili powder to coat evenly; sprinkle on the oil and toss again.
Arrange the potato strips in a single layer on baking sheet.
Bake for 20 minutes, then turn and continue baking until crisp and browned—about 20 minutes more.
Sprinkle with salt when done.
Makes 4 servings.

Papas a la Juancainino

This dish is from Judy Etchenique, Linda Lamacki's sister. Linda is one of the faithful volunteers at the Chicago branch of Jews for Jesus. Although she and her family live in Chicago, her sister Judy settled in Brazil. Once, when Judy was visiting, the entire branch staff was invited to Linda's house for dinner. Judy made Papas a la Juancainino. It is not a Brazilian dish, but a Bolivian one.

When we enjoy ethnic dishes such as this, we can't help but think of what we're going to eat at the Marriage Supper of the Lamb. After all, there will be people from "every tribe and nation" seated at the same table. Do you think we'll have matzoh ball soup? Perhaps there will be Papas a la Juancainino.

Large, whole, boiled potatoes—1 per person
hard-boiled eggs
tomatoes, quartered

Peanut sauce:
½   pound peanut butter (not chunky)
½   pound ricotta cheese
½   teaspoon salt
½   teaspoon dried red peppers
½   teaspoon chopped jalapeno peppers

Blend all sauce ingredients in a blender or food processor. If sauce is too thick, add a little milk.

Heat the peanut sauce slowly in a saucepan.
When hot, pour over large, whole, peeled boiled potatoes that have been arranged on a platter of lettuce, along with hard-cooked eggs and tomatoes.
This serves a large group of about ten adults.

Potato Paprikash (from a Jewish Mother)

Part of a Jewish mother's job description is that she loves to see her children eat. You don't have to be Jewish to make this recipe, or even a mother, but those you serve it to will love to eat it.

  3   large potatoes, peeled and diced
 1/4   cup green pepper, diced
  1   small onion, diced
  2   cubes or 2 teaspoons chicken bouillon
 1/2   teaspoon paprika
       salt and pepper
  1   tablespoon margarine

Sauté onion and green pepper in small amount of margarine in large frying pan. Add potatoes (raw) and remaining ingredients. Almost cover with water. Cover pan and cook until potatoes are soft. Makes 3-4 servings.

Sweet Potatoes in Orange Halves

  6   medium sweet potatoes, baked in jackets
  2   tablespoons butter or margarine plus 1-2 tablespoons more
  6   navel oranges
 1/2   teaspoon salt
  3   tablespoons brown sugar

Peel cooked potatoes, mash with two tablespoons butter or margarine in large bowl; add salt and brown sugar and mix well. Cut oranges in half; remove fruit (save it for another time). Fill each orange half with mashed potato mixture; sprinkle with brown sugar and dot with additional butter or margarine. Place in muffin tins. Bake in 350° oven for 30 minutes. Makes 12 servings.

Two from E.Z. (Ellen Zaretsky):

Potato Pancakes

  6   potatoes, raw, medium-size
  1   medium onion
 3/4   cup matzoh meal
  2   eggs
 1/2   teaspoon salt
 1/4   teaspoon pepper

Grate potatoes and drain well in colander. Add grated onion, matzoh meal, eggs, salt and pepper. Drop by large tablespoons onto hot, greased griddle or frying pan. Cook until crusty brown; turn and repeat on other side. Makes 1 dozen. Serve with applesauce.

Candied Sweet Potatoes

6	medium-sized sweet potatoes, peeled and cooked
1	cup brown sugar, packed
1/4	cup butter or margarine
1/4	cup water
1/2	teaspoon salt
1/4	cup walnuts, chopped (optional)
2	whole cloves (optional)

Arrange cooked potatoes, cut in half lengthwise, in greased baking dish. Combine rest of ingredients (except nuts) in saucepan; boil together for 5 minutes. Pour this mixture over potatoes; top with nuts. Bake at 375° for 30 minutes, basting occasionally with liquid in pan. Makes 6 servings

If made in skillet: Cut cooked potatoes in half lengthwise. Combine remaining ingredients in large skillet (except nuts); boil together for 5 minutes. Arrange potatoes in syrup. Sprinkle nuts over top. Simmer 20 minutes, turning and basting occasionally.

Ecuadorian Potato Dumplings with Cheese

5	large potatoes
3	whole green onions
	salt
1	tablespoon solid vegetable shortening
1	egg
1	teaspoon solid vegetable shortening
	achiote annatto (see Note) or ground paprika
8	ounces cream cheese
	butter or margarine

Peel and quarter potatoes; cover with water in large pot and cook with whole green onions, salt and 1 tablespoon vegetable shortening. When done, drain off water; remove onion and mash potatoes. Finely chop cooked green onions when done; add to potatoes with egg and salt. In small frying pan mix together 1 teaspoon vegetable shortening melted with 1/2 teaspoon achiote annatto. Cook several minutes; remove kernels; blend 1/2 teaspoon achiote annatto mixture into potato mixture.

Potato mixture should now be a nice yellowish-orange color. Place some of this mixture in the palm of your hand; place a small bit of cream cheese over this; put more potato over the cream cheese (like you're making a dumpling). Carefully place dumplings in a frying pan in which a small amount of butter or margarine has been melted. Fry over medium heat until golden in color on both sides.

Makes about 1 dozen dumplings. These are good when served with finely chopped lettuce, beet and carrot salad and slices of tomatoes and avocado on the side.

Note: Achiote annatto is a spice that can be found in specialty shops or Spanish grocery stores. Paprika can be substituted for it.

Gartman's Parmesan Potato Bake

$1/4$ cup butter or margarine
$1/2$ teaspoon salt
$1/4$ teaspoon pepper
 3   medium baking potatoes, unpeeled, cut into $1/8$" thick slices
 2   tablespoons grated Parmesan cheese
 2   tablespoons red pepper, chopped (or canned pimento)
 2   tablespoons fresh parsley, chopped

Heat oven to 350°. In ungreased 9"x13" baking dish, melt butter in oven (5-7 minutes). Stir in salt and pepper. Stir in potatoes until coated with butter. Cover dish with foil and bake for 30 minutes. Remove foil; sprinkle with Parmesan cheese. Continue baking, uncovered, for 20-30 minutes or until potatoes are crisp-tender. Sprinkle with red pepper and parsley before serving.
Makes 5 servings.

German Fried Potatoes

Cut cold, boiled, peeled potatoes into thick slices (1 potato per person). Melt butter in large frying pan and add 1 finely chopped onion; sauté lightly and add potatoes. Season well with salt and pepper. Turn a few times with spatula until slightly browned. Sprinkle with grated Swiss cheese before serving.

Space Potatoes (Out of this World)

8-10   medium potatoes, quartered and unpeeled
  1   stick ($1/2$ cup) butter or margarine
  1   pint half-and-half
  1   tablespoon salt
$1/4$ cup Parmesan cheese, grated
3-4   ounces sharp cheddar cheese, grated
     pepper

Cook potatoes in water to cover until done.
Cool overnight.
Peel potatoes and grate in food processor.
Put in greased 9"x13" pan.
Melt together butter or margarine with half-and-half.
Stir in salt and mix well.
Pour this mixture over potatoes.
Sprinkle with Parmesan and cheddar cheeses.
Bake at 350° for 1 hour, or for 1 $1/2$ hours if frozen before cooking.
Makes 10-12 servings.

Section Three–Rice and Beans

Rijattafel (Curry with Coconut)

Curry is to Jews (or anyone else) in India what kosher hot dogs are to Jews in America, a fact of life.

- 2 cups grated, unsweetened coconut
- 4 cups milk, scalded
- 1 tablespoon butter or margarine
- 1/2 cup onion, chopped
-   dash ground ginger
- 1 clove garlic, chopped
- 1 1/2 tablespoons curry powder
- 1 cup chicken broth or bouillon
- 1 tablespoon flour
- 1 tablespoon cornstarch
- 3 cups cooked chicken, fish, veal, mushrooms or vegetables
- 2 cups cooked rice

Add coconut to hot milk. Let stand for 2 hours in a cool place. Melt butter or margarine and sauté onion in it until light brown. Add a dash of ginger, chopped garlic and curry powder to onion mixture. Drain coconut and add to this mixture. Add chicken stock or bouillon.

Combine flour with cornstarch; mix with 3 tablespoons of above mixture.

Heat remaining mixture and stir in the coconut milk and starch-paste. Cook and stir sauce until it is hot and thickened. Season to taste.

Add cooked chicken, fish, veal, mushrooms or vegetables to the sauce; heat gently. Serve over cooked rice. Makes 4 servings.

Rice and Vegetables Casserole

- 2 cups white rice, uncooked
- 1 (6-ounce) can water chestnuts, sliced
- 1 (10-ounce) can bamboo shoots, sliced
- 3 (10 1/2-ounce) cans condensed mushroom soup
- 2 packages (1 1/2-ounces each) dry onion soup mix
- 1 stick (1/2 cup) margarine
- 1 package (16-ounce) frozen mixed vegetables.

Combine all ingredients except mixed vegetables in large mixing bowl. Place in greased 3-quart casserole. Bake, covered, at 350° for 50 minutes. Stir in vegetables and bake 15 minutes more. Makes 6-8 servings.

Baked Beans from Albuquerque

1 (31-ounce) can vegetarian baked beans
3/4 cup brown sugar
1 teaspoon brown sugar
6 slices raw turkey bacon, cut in small pieces
1/2 cup catsup
1 large onion, diced
1/4 cup dark molasses
1/4 teaspoon salt
1 teaspoon liquid smoke

Combine all ingredients well and put in a greased casserole and bake at 300° for 2-3 hours.
Makes 4-6 servings.

Coconut Garbanzo Rice

This recipe is straight out of the hippie generation, as are many of the original Jews for Jesus.

2 cups brown rice
3/4 cup grated coconut, unsweetened
1 teaspoon salt
1 cup canned chickpeas (garbanzo beans)
4 tablespoons butter or margarine
1 onion, sliced
1 green pepper, sliced
1 teaspoon mustard seed
1 teaspoon turmeric
1 teaspoon ground cardamom
1/2 teaspoon ground cloves
1/2 teaspoon cinnamon
1/2 cup raisins

Bring 4 1/4 cups water to a boil and stir in first four ingredients.
Cover and lower heat; let simmer about 45 minutes.
Remove from heat but do not remove cover.
Meanwhile melt butter or margarine in small frying pan and sauté onion and green pepper; cook until soft.
Add seasonings; cover and let steam with raisins.
When raisins are plump, stir all into cooked rice mixture and mix well.
Makes 6 servings.

Chinese Rice

3 strips turkey bacon, raw
1/2 cup green onions, sliced
1/2-3/4 cup celery, sliced
1 (4-ounce) can mushroom pieces, drained
2 eggs
1/4-1/2 cup soy sauce
3-4 cups cooked rice
leftover cooked chicken or beef, chopped

Fry bacon until crisp; drain and crumble on paper towels.
Sauté sliced onion and celery in 1 tablespoon bacon fat until tender; add canned mushrooms and sauté a few minutes more.
Make an omelet of the 2 eggs in a separate frying pan; when cooked, slice into thin strips.
Add vegetable mixture and sliced omelet to cooked rice in large saucepan.
Add soy sauce to taste.
Heat over low flame, adding cooked meat and stirring well.
Makes 6-8 servings.

Rice-Tuna Bake

2 cups cooked rice
2 (7-ounce) cans tuna fish
1 (10-ounce) package frozen peas
1 (10 3/4-ounce) can condensed cream of mushroom soup
1/4 cup onion, chopped
salt and pepper
1 cup American or cheddar cheese, grated
paprika

Place cooked rice in a buttered casserole dish.
Cover with well-drained tuna chunks.
Cover with frozen peas.
In a saucepan, heat cream of mushroom soup with 1/2 can water;
add chopped onion and salt and pepper to taste.
Heat; pour over rice layers.
Bake 15-20 minutes at 350°; top with grated cheddar or
American cheese and sprinkle with paprika.
Bake 15-20 minutes more.
Makes 4-6 servings.

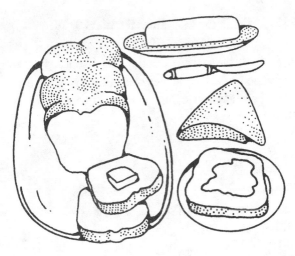

If You Have Bread, You Have a Meal

If you've grown up in a Jewish home in New York City, you're familiar with that New York staple of life, rye bread with caraway seeds. This is not ordinary rye bread. The crust is shiny and crispy and chewy all at the same time. The bread is redolent with the fragrance of caraway seeds. You can get the bread without seeds, too, but it's just not the same. You ask the salesperson to slice it, and when it's handed over the counter, it's wrapped in a crinkly white paper bag. Good boys and girls who are sent to the bakery to purchase the bread for Sunday afternoon lunch are favored with a special treat: They get to eat the heel of the bread on the way home. Now, the heel, or the ends, of the bread are the best part. They are the most crispy, the most chewy and the freshest piece of all. Jewish children grow up with all sorts of memories; some of us in Jews for Jesus have fond memories of eating rye bread on the way home.

Is it possible to find good Jewish rye bread in other parts of the country? Where can you find your own slice of rye bread heaven? Well, there is an outstanding recipe for rye bread in this chapter. Perhaps you can make your own memories from it.

While we may know about rye bread, we Jews for Jesus don't know much about gardening. We've been raised in cities like New York and Los Angeles, areas hardly conducive to growing anything green. One of the staff missionaries, a New Yorker by birth, was transferred to the Midwest. Her new house had an area in the backyard that had been plotted out by the previous owner to be used as a vegetable garden. Our missionary reported that she was so excited, she promptly bought and planted ten little zucchini plants. Over the summer they grew into ten huge zucchini plants, and the zucchinis were everywhere. This smart missionary promptly learned a lot about cooking with zucchini and vowed never to plant more than two or three of any type of vegetable ever again! In this chapter you'll find her recipe for zucchini bread, which is good enough to knock your socks off. Your children won't even know they're eating anything healthy, since the zucchini seems to disappear into the bread as it bakes.

This chapter is dedicated to all bread bakers everywhere.

Pineapple Zucchini Bread to Nosh on

Says Lori McHugh, "In my house, we had the tradition of inviting friends over after dinner for what we called 'coffee and . . .' The 'and' was some type of cake or sweet bread, enjoyed during several hours of schmoozing (talking and passing the time). This bread is a good nosh (snack) to schmooze over."

3	eggs
³/₄	cup vegetable oil
1 ³/₄	cups sugar
2	teaspoons vanilla extract
2	cups coarsely shredded, unpeeled zucchini
1	(8-ounce) can crushed pineapple, drained
3	cups flour, sifted
2	teaspoons baking soda
1	teaspoon salt
½	teaspoon baking powder
1 ½	teaspoons cinnamon
³/₄	teaspoon nutmeg
1	cup walnuts, chopped

In a large bowl, beat eggs; add oil, sugar and vanilla; continue beating until mixture is thick and foamy. Stir in zucchini and pineapple. In a separate bowl, stir together flour, baking soda, salt, baking powder, cinnamon, nutmeg and walnuts. Stir gently into zucchini mixture until just blended. Spoon batter equally into two greased and floured 9"x5" loaf pans. Bake in 350° oven for 1 hour or until toothpick inserted in center comes out clean. Let cool in pans 10 minutes, then turn out onto racks to cool. Makes 2 loaves.

Sesame Wheat Germ Cornbread

This is a health food enthusiast's version of an old Southern favorite.

1 ½	cups flour, sifted
½	cup sugar
1 ½	teaspoons salt
1 ¼	teaspoons baking soda
2	cups cornmeal
1	cup wheat germ
½	cup sesame seeds, toasted
2	cups buttermilk
½	cup vegetable oil
2	eggs, lightly beaten

In a large bowl, stir together flour, sugar, salt and baking soda until well blended. Mix in cornmeal, wheat germ and sesame seeds. In a separate bowl, mix together buttermilk, oil and eggs. Stir liquid mixture into dry ingredients until well blended. Pour into greased 9"x5" loaf pan. Bake in 375° oven for 35 minutes or until a toothpick inserted in center comes out clean. Let cool in pan 5 minutes; then turn out onto a rack to cool completely. Makes 1 large loaf.

Cornbread ala Black

From Marcia Goldstein's family (the Black's) we get this wonderful recipe for lovely, golden cornbread.

2	tablespoons butter, margarine or shortening
1 1/4	cups flour
3/4	cup cornmeal (white or yellow)
4	teaspoons baking powder
1	cup milk
1	egg
1/2	teaspoon salt

Melt the 2 tablespoons butter, margarine or shortening in a 9x5" loaf pan, and grease pan with it. Mix the remaining ingredients together. Bake at 375° for 30 minutes or until a toothpick inserted in center comes out clean. Let cool in pan 5 minutes; turn out onto rack to cool completely. Makes 1 loaf.

Tin Can Date Nut Bread

So called because it's baked in an empty coffee can, but there's nothing metallic about it!

1/2	cup packed brown sugar
1/3	cup shortening, margarine or butter
1	egg
1/2	teaspoon vanilla extract
1 1/3	cups flour
1/2	teaspoon salt
1/2	teaspoon baking soda
1/2	teaspoon nutmeg
1/8	teaspoon ground cloves
3/4	cup milk
2/3	cup pitted dates, chopped
1/4	cup walnuts, chopped

Cream together brown sugar and shortening, margarine or butter.
Add egg and vanilla extract.
In separate bowl, stir together flour, salt, baking soda, nutmeg and cloves.
Add milk to creamed mixture.
Mix in flour mixture, dates and walnuts.
Pour into 2 greased and floured 1-pound coffee cans.
Bake at 350° for 45-50 minutes.
Cool slightly before removing from cans.
Cool on cake rack.
Wrap in aluminum foil and chill overnight.
Makes 2 loaves.

Pumpkin Bread

3	cups sugar
1	teaspoon baking powder
1	teaspoon each ground cloves, nutmeg and cinnamon
3 1/2	cups flour
2	teaspoons baking soda
1 1/2	teaspoons salt
1	cup oil
1	cup buttermilk or plain yogurt
2	cups canned pumpkin (not pumpkin pie filling)
4	eggs
1	cup walnuts or pecans, chopped
1	cup pitted dates, chopped

Mix together sugar, baking powder, cloves, nutmeg, cinnamon, flour, baking soda and salt in a large bowl. Add oil, buttermilk or yogurt, eggs and pumpkin; mix well.

Stir in chopped nuts and dates.

Bake at 350° in 2 greased and floured 9"x5" loaf pans for 1 hour, or until cake tester inserted in center comes out clean.

Glaze with the following:

Glaze:

1	cup sugar
1	teaspoon honey
1/2	teaspoon baking soda
4	tablespoons butter or margarine
1/2	cup buttermilk
1	teaspoon vanilla extract

Bring all glaze ingredients except extract to a boil in medium saucepan.

Stir in vanilla extract.

Pour over bread while still in pans and put them back in oven for 5 minutes (this tends to run over the sides so you may want to put aluminum foil under the pans).

When slightly cooled, remove loaves from pans.

Makes 2 loaves.

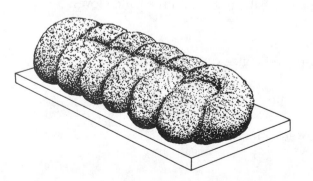

Zucchini Bread ala Abundance

This recipe will come in handy if you goof and plant too many zucchini plants in your garden.

3	eggs
2	cups sugar
1	cup oil
2	cups zucchini, unpeeled and grated
1	teaspoon vanilla or lemon extract
3	cups flour
1	teaspoon salt
1	teaspoon baking soda
1	teaspoon baking powder
2	teaspoons cinnamon
1/2	cup pecans, chopped
1	cup raisins

Beat eggs until foamy, add sugar, oil, zucchini and extract; mix well. Sift the 5 dry ingredients together and add to egg mixture. Stir in nuts and raisins. Divide batter into two greased and floured 9"x5" loaf pans. Bake in preheated 325° oven for 1 hour, or until done. Remove from pans when cool. Makes 2 loaves.

The Best Cranberry Nut Bread

In New England, where Janie-sue Wertheim was raised, it's easy to find cranberries in the supermarket all year round. Since cranberries are more of a seasonal item in most other places, Janie-sue's offered this recipe made with dried apricots, as well. If you use apricots and they are very dry, pour 1 cup of boiling water over them and let them sit for 45 minutes before you add them to the batter (drain well before adding).

2	cups flour, sifted
1	cup sugar
1 1/2	teaspoons baking powder
1	teaspoon salt
1/2	teaspoon baking soda
1	cup fresh cranberries, coarsely chopped
	(or 1 cup chopped, dried apricots plus 1 cup boiling water)
1	cup chopped nuts (see Note)
1/4	cup shortening
1	teaspoon grated orange peel
3/4	cup orange juice
1	egg, beaten

Sift together the dry ingredients; cut in shortening. Combine peel, juice and egg. Add to dry ingredients, mixing just to moisten. Fold in fruit and nuts. Put in a greased and floured 9"x5" loaf pan. Bake at 350° oven for 1 hour or until cake tester inserted in center comes out clean. Cool and wrap in aluminum foil; store overnight before serving. Makes 1 loaf.

Note: Janie-sue uses chopped walnuts in the cranberry bread and chopped pecans in the apricot bread.

Real Rye Bread

Blend:
- 2   cups rye flour
- 1/4   cup unsweetened cocoa
- 1   tablespoon salt

Dissolve 2 packages dry yeast in 1/2 cup warm water.

Combine in bowl:
- 1/2   cup dark molasses
- 1   cup warm water
- 1/4   cup caraway seeds

Add flour mixture, dissolved yeast, 1 tablespoon butter or margarine and 1 cup white flour to molasses mixture. Beat until batter is smooth.

Stir in enough white flour to make a smooth dough (about 2 3/4 to 3 cups more).

Knead about 10 minutes. Let rise in a warm place until double (about 1 hour). Punch down; shape into 2 round loaves and place on greased cookie sheet. Let rise until double again (50-60 minutes). Bake at 375° for 35-40 minutes. Let cool completely on racks. Makes 2 loaves.

Marion's Dill Bread

Curt and Marion Shacklett are good friends from Tulsa Bible Church. Jhan Moskowitz was once invited to be the speaker for their retreat weekend. After giving his morning teaching, Jhan and Curt decided to go canoeing, while Marion took me to a down-home, hillbilly Arkansas craft festival. Upon our return, we saw Jhan's clothing hanging out on the line to dry. It seems that the two men managed to overturn their canoe while it was still tied to the dock. This story will certainly go down in T.B.C.'s history. And to think, Jhan once claimed to be a pirate . . .

Marion's recipe for dill bread is sure to bring infamous reviews in your house.

- 2   packages yeast, sprinkled over 1/2 cup warm water
- 2   eggs, beaten
- 2   cups cottage cheese
- 4   tablespoons honey
- 2   tablespoons instant minced onion
- 2   tablespoons butter or margarine
- 4   teaspoons dill seed
- 2   teaspoons salt
- 1/2   teaspoon baking soda
- 5   cups flour

When yeast is dissolved, mix in eggs until well blended. Heat together the next seven ingredients until warm; mix together with yeast/egg mixture. Add the flour to form a stiff dough. Let stand in warm place until doubled in bulk. Punch down and place in 2 well-greased loaf pans. Let rise until doubled in bulk. Bake in 350° oven 30-35 minutes. Lightly butter top when done. Makes 2 loaves.

The Challah That Almost Didn't Make It

It's not that this recipe almost failed; it's that it almost failed to make its way into this cookbook! Challah is perhaps one of the most traditional of all Jewish foods. It is a braided egg bread that accompanies the Friday night dinner that ushers in the Jewish Sabbath. A special prayer is chanted to give God thanks for giving us bread from the earth.

But challah can be enjoyed any day of the week. In fact, you definitely do not have to be Jewish to either bake it or eat it. Cynthia Strull, whose husband Dan leads a messianic congregation in Chicago, submitted this recipe. Of course there's a story that goes with it:

"When Dan and I moved to Columbia, South Carolina to attend Bible college, we had culture shock. There weren't a lot of Jewish people there; in fact, several of Dan's classmates told him that he was the first Jewish person they had met! I couldn't find challah in the stores, so I started experimenting with recipes and began baking my own each week. I didn't realize then that it would become a special tradition that I would eventually share with each of our children as we would measure, mix, knead and braid our challah bread on Fridays. Even the simplest Sabbath meal seems special with the fragrance of this bread filling the house, and little eyes shining with pride as we pass the bread around the table."

Do you know what a Proverbs 31 woman is like? Thank you, Cynthia, for giving us that picture.

1	cup milk
6	tablespoons butter or margarine
1/4-1/3	cup sugar (use the lesser amount if you don't like your bread sweet)
1	package active dry yeast
3	eggs
1	teaspoon salt
4-5	cups unbleached, all-purpose flour
1	tablespoon cold water

Bring milk, 4 tablespoons butter and the sugar just to boil in a saucepan. Immediately remove from heat; pour into large mixing bowl and let cool to lukewarm. (Says Cynthia: "I have placed ice cubes in a slightly larger dish and placed it underneath the bowl with the milk mixture to hasten the cooling process. By stirring frequently it will cool. Take the slightly melted ice water and fix yourself a glass of tea while you're baking.")

Stir yeast into cooled milk mixture. Let stand for 10 minutes. It will get foamy. Beat 2 of the eggs in another small bowl. Add salt to beaten eggs; stir into milk and yeast mixture.

Stir in 3 to 4 cups of flour in to egg/milk mixture. Add flour 1 cup at a time, until you have a sticky dough. Sprinkle flour on a work surface and turn dough onto it (at this point you can stop and wash and dry your bowl, or use another clean one). Smear the 2 tablespoons of reserved butter or margarine around the inside of the bowl and set aside).

Sprinkle additional flour over the dough and begin kneading, adding flour as necessary. Knead until you have a smooth, non-sticky, elastic dough.

Place dough in the greased bowl, turning dough to coat with butter. Cover top of bowl with towel and place somewhere out of a draft where the dough can rise undisturbed for 1 ½ hours. The dough should triple in bulk. You can test the dough by poking 2 fingers lightly in the center. If the finger holes stay depressed, and it looks like a bowling ball, it's ready.

Punch down the dough and turn it onto a floured surface. To make 2 loaves, cut dough into 2 equal parts (work with 1 half at a time). Cut each half into thirds. Roll out into "snakes" about 18" long. Braid snakes together; pinch ends together and tucking them under. Transfer each loaf onto a lightly greased baking sheet. Cover with clean dish towel and let rise about 1 hour.

Preheat oven to 350°. Separate the yolk from the white of the third egg; discard or save white. Beat egg yolk with one tablespoon cold water. Lightly brush the egg wash evenly over the loaves of bread. Set baking sheet on middle rack of oven. Bake 30 minutes (or less) until golden brown. Lightly tap with knife across top of loaf to test for doneness. It will sound hollow when done. Cool completely before eating. Makes 2 loaves.

Baked Apple Pancake

4	large (or 7-8 small) baking apples
1	cup milk
1	cup flour
2	tablespoons sugar
	dash salt
6	eggs
	cinnamon/sugar mixture
	butter or margarine

Grease a 9"x13" pan. Peel, core and thinly slice apples and place in pan. In medium bowl, beat together milk, flour, sugar, salt and eggs. Pour over apples. Bake in preheated 500° oven for 12 minutes. Sprinkle with cinnamon/sugar mixture, dot with butter, and bake 5 minutes more. Serve warm. Makes 6 servings.

German Egg Pancakes

1	cup flour
1 ½	cups milk
3	eggs
	dash salt
	favorite flavor jelly
	sugar for sprinkling

Beat together flour, milk, eggs and salt in medium bowl. Lightly grease small (8"-10") frying pan or crepe pan. Heat over medium flame until hot. Use small amount of batter to make a thin pancake, tilting pan so that batter covers bottom. When golden brown, turn and lightly fry on other side. Remove from pan and spread with a thin layer of jelly; roll up and sprinkle with sugar. Makes 12 pancakes.

Panqueques con Dulce de Leche (Crepes Filled with Milk Jam)

Zhava Glaser says that this recipe works best when the directions are followed exactly. When you get to the filling, you may not believe what you're reading. But just follow the directions explicitly, and you won't have a problem.

Panqueques:
- 4 eggs
- 1 cup flour
- 2 tablespoons sugar
- 1 cup milk
- 1/4 cup water
- 1 tablespoon butter or margarine, melted

In medium bowl, beat eggs; slowly add flour, sugar, milk and water. Beat until smooth; add melted butter or margarine. (This can be prepared in a blender: Blend all ingredients for about 1 minute; scrape jar, blend another 30 seconds until well-blended). Let mixture stand for about an hour.

Grease a skillet or crepe pan with a little butter or margarine over medium-high flame.
Drop in 2-3 tablespoons batter.
Quickly swirl batter around to cover bottom of pan with a thin layer, as you lift the pan above the flame.
Lower pan and cook until bottom is browned;
turn carefully and brown other side of panqueque for a few seconds.
Stack panqueques onto a plate.

Dulce de leche filling:
- 1 large can sweetened condensed milk

Quickly remove wrapper from can so you don't see how many calories it contains!
DO NOT OPEN CAN, but drop sealed can into a pot of cold water to cover.
Place over low heat.
Bring slowly to a boil and cook for 2 hours (make sure there's always enough water to cover can; if not, add more water and turn can occasionally).
Remove from flame and let can cool in water overnight, or for several hours.
Open can, spread over individual panqueques, roll them up, and enjoy!

Zhava says, "Dulce de leche is the favorite treat among South American children, ages 1-99! It's put on everything, from morning toast to sponge cake, but one of the best combinations is as a filling for panqueques. To do this, spread the dulce de leche thinly over a panqueque, roll up the pancake as you would a jelly roll. Then eat! But be careful, it tends to drip out the other side! Have plenty of napkins on hand!"

Orange Whole Wheat Pancakes

2 eggs
$1/4$ cup salad oil
2 cups whole wheat flour
$1/2$ teaspoon baking soda
$1/2$ teaspoon salt
$1^1/2$-2 cups orange juice

Beat the eggs and oil together. Add the dry ingredients and gradually add the orange juice until you have a batter with the consistency you like. Fry the pancakes on a medium-hot griddle and serve immediately. Makes 12-14 pancakes.

Serve with sour cream or yogurt mixed with a little honey. For an interesting variation, add a few teaspoons of ground walnuts to the batter.

Thanksgiving-Through-Christmas Bran Muffins

The batter for these muffins will keep in the refrigerator from Thanksgiving all the way through Christmas, hence the name.

1 cup margarine or Crisco
2 cups sugar
4 eggs, separated
1 quart buttermilk
5 cups flour
1 teaspoon salt

Mix these ingredients together in a large bowl.
2 cups boiling water
5 teaspoons baking soda (measured carefully)

Combine and cool; add to the shortening/buttermilk/flour mixture.
4 cups All-Bran cereal
2 cups 40% Bran Flakes
2 cups chopped, pitted dates
1 cup walnuts, chopped

Crumble together, then add to above mixture.
Store in airtight, wide-mouth jars (about 5) or in covered Tupperware container.
To bake, fill greased muffin pans $1/2$ full with mixture.
Bake 15-20 minutes at 350°.
Remainder of mixture can be kept refrigerated up to 6 weeks.
Makes 5 dozen muffins

Mr. P.'s Never-Fail Pancakes

This is Ellen Zaretsky's recipe, which was given to her by her sixth grade science teacher. It's such an easy recipe, there's very little that's scientific about it.

1	egg
1	cup buttermilk
1	teaspoon oil
2	tablespoons sugar
	pinch salt
1	cup flour
1	teaspoon baking soda
1	teaspoon baking powder

Combine the egg, buttermilk, oil, sugar and salt in a large bowl.
Add the dry ingredients and mix well.
Fry the pancakes on a medium-hot griddle or in an electric frying pan set at 380°.
Makes 8-10 pancakes.

Of Challah and Bananas (French Toast with a Twist)

This is not your typical recipe for French toast. In many Jewish homes, challah is eaten with the Friday evening meal. On Sunday morning, if you're fortunate, there will be enough challah left over to make this special French toast. It will be a special hit with the children.

1	egg
$1/2$	banana, sliced
$1/2$	teaspoon cinnamon
3	slices challah (or whole wheat bread)
2	teaspoons butter, margarine or oil
	maple syrup, applesauce or yogurt

Put egg, banana and cinnamon in blender; blend until smooth.
Pour batter into flat bowl.
Melt butter or margarine in large frying pan over medium flame.
Dip slices of challah or wheat bread in egg mixture to coat on both sides, and place gently in frying pan.
Lower heat and cook until lightly browned on both sides.
Serve immediately with syrup, applesauce or yogurt.
Makes 2 servings.

Emily's Banana Muffins

Jhan Moskowitz once had a wonderful office manager, Emily, at the Chicago branch office. One of the reasons Emily was so wonderful was that she had a heart for missions. She was perfect for the job because she understood the Jews for Jesus vision for reaching Jewish people with the Gospel. But one day, something not so wonderful happened to Jhan and the Chicago branch: Emily and her husband Terry felt called to go to Russia to preach the Gospel there. Before she left, she gave us this recipe for muffins, which she had brought to the office from time to time. We miss you Emily!

1/2	cup butter or margarine
1	cup sugar
1	cup mashed bananas (2 or 3 medium)
1	egg
1	teaspoon baking soda, dissolved in 2 tablespoons hot water
1/2	teaspoon salt
1 1/2	cups flour

Cream butter or margarine with sugar in large bowl.
Stir in mashed bananas, egg, baking soda, salt and flour, beating until barely mixed.
Fill muffin tins half full with batter.
Bake in preheated 375° oven for 20 minutes. Makes 12 muffins..

Apple Muffins

2	cups flour
2	teaspoons baking powder
3/4	teaspoon salt
2	tablespoons sugar
2	tablespoons butter or margarine
1	cup apples, peeled and chopped
1	egg, beaten
1/2	cup milk
2	tablespoons sugar, mixed with 1/2 teaspoon cinnamon
1/2	cup apple, peeled and diced

Mix together flour with baking powder, salt and sugar.
Cut in butter or margarine with fork or pastry blender.
Add 1 cup peeled and chopped apples.
Lightly and quickly add egg and milk.
Fill greased muffin tins 2/3 full. Place some diced apple on top of batter, sprinkle with cinnamon/sugar mixture.
Bake at 400° for 20 minutes. Makes 12 muffins.

Lowfat Fruit and Bran Muffins

Diane Cohen tracked down this recipe at the last minute so that it could be included before the cookbook went to press.

Preheat oven to 350°.

1	cup oat bran
³/₄	cup wheat bran
³/₄	cup whole wheat flour
1	cup mixed dried fruit - any combination you prefer, chopped
¹/₄	cup walnuts, chopped
1	teaspoon cinnamon
1	teaspoon baking powder
¹/₂	teaspoon baking soda
	pinch salt

Mix above ingredients together in large bowl. In separate bowl whisk together:

2	large egg whites
1 ¹/₄	cups applesauce
¹/₂	cup brown sugar, packed
¹/₂	cup plain, nonfat yogurt

Add to dry ingredients, stirring just until blended. Spoon into greased muffin cups or paper liners. Bake at 350° for 30-35 minutes. Makes 12-14 muffins.

Blueberry Muffins

1³/₄	cup cake flour, sifted
2	teaspoons baking powder
¹/₂	teaspoon salt
¹/₄	cup butter or margarine
¹/₄	cup sugar
2	eggs
³/₄	cup milk
1¹/₂	cups blueberries, washed
	grated rind of ¹/₂ lemon

Mix together flour, baking powder and salt. In separate bowl cream butter or margarine with sugar; add eggs, then quickly add in flour mixture with milk. Fold in blueberries and lemon rind. Fill greased muffin tins ²/₃ full. Bake at 400° for 20 minutes. Makes 12 muffins.

Deep Dish Pizza, Fast and Fun

> 2 cans refrigerated French bread (in refrigerated biscuit section)
> olive oil
> 1 (28-ounce) can sliced, stewed tomatoes, drained
> 1½ pounds mozzarella cheese, sliced thick
> ½ pound mushrooms, sliced (optional)
> ½ pound ground beef or turkey sausage (crumbled), cooked
> 1 cup broccoli or spinach, cooked and chopped

Remove the dough from the containers (do not unroll) and set on dry tabletop or wooden cutting board to warm to room temperature; let rise slightly. Carefully unroll dough. Grease a 9"x13" baking dish with olive oil. Gently press one rectangular sheet of dough in pan, making sure it covers the sides. Spread ½ the cheese slices over dough. Place tomatoes on top. Add optional ingredients, if you like. Cover with remaining cheese and top with second rectangle of dough. Seal dough around edges. Bake preheated 350° oven for 50 minutes. Allow to cool 20 minutes before serving. Makes 6-8 servings.

Leah's Pizza

Leah San Hamel is both beautiful AND a good cook. Her beauty comes from her love for God. Her cooking skills come from where? It doesn't matter; just make this pizza (or its variation) and enjoy.

Dough:

> 3 cups unbleached flour
> ½ stick margarine, softened
> ½ teaspoon salt
> 1 package dry yeast and a pinch of sugar, mixed in 1 cup warm water
> olive oil
> 1 teaspoon oregano
> 1 cup Romano cheese, grated

Sauce:
> 1 clove garlic, chopped
> 1 small onion, chopped
> 1 (6-ounce) can tomato paste
> 1 tomato paste can water
> 1 (8-ounce) can whole, peeled tomatoes, undrained
> salt, pepper
> ½ teaspoon basil
> 1 (16-ounce) can whole, peeled tomatoes, drained
> 1½ cups Mozzarella, grated

Mix flour, margarine and salt together in large bowl. Add the yeast/water mixture and form dough into soft ball. If dough is too moist, add a little more flour and gradually form into a soft, stretchy dough. Put dough into a clean bowl; cover bowl with clean cloth and set aside in a warm, dark place to rise.

After dough rises, punch it down and spread it out on a greased pizza pan (about 12" in diameter). Drizzle $1/2$ tablespoon olive oil over dough and spread lightly with fingertips. Sprinkle with oregano and grated Romano cheese.

Heat 1 tablespoon olive oil in small saucepan over low heat and sauté chopped garlic and onion until lightly browned. Add tomato paste and water, small can tomatoes and blend together well. Add salt and pepper to taste; add basil and stir well. Remove from heat.

Spread tomato sauce over dough. Cut each canned tomato into small chunks with kitchen scissors and place evenly over pizza dough. Sprinkle with grated Mozzarella.

Bake in preheated 425° oven for approximately 20 minutes, or until lightly browned and bubbly. Makes 6 servings.

Variation—White Pizza: Using dough as prepared above, spread in greased 9"x13" pan. Sprinkle with same amounts of oregano and grated Romano as above.

Sauce:

1	tablespoon olive oil
1	large onion, chopped
1	large clove garlic, chopped
	salt and pepper to taste
$1/2$	teaspoon basil
1	cup fontinella cheese, grated

Sauté onion and garlic in olive oil. Add salt and pepper to taste, and $1/2$ teaspoon basil. Spread evenly over dough. Crumble fontinella cheese over top; press lightly into dough. Place in preheated 425° oven for approximately 20 minutes, or until bubbly. Makes 6-8 servings.

Mandlach (Soup Nuts)

3	medium eggs
2	tablespoons vegetable oil
2	cups flour
1	teaspoon salt

Combine all ingredients in medium bowl, beat well with wooden spoon.

Knead on lightly floured board until well blended.

Divide dough into 3 parts and roll into 3/8" ropes.

Cut into $1/2$" pieces, place in well-greased roasting pan and bake in 375° oven until golden brown (shaking pan occasionally so that nuts brown evenly).

Serve with chicken soup.

Makes 10-12 servings.

A Little Girl's Topping for Vegetables

Jessie Moskowitz made a real mess in the kitchen while concocting this recipe, but she had a lot of fun doing it! It is a good topping for vegetables, especially cooked carrots or corn.

$1/2$ cup Cheddar cheese, grated
$1/2$ cup popcorn, popped and grated (try a hand-held cheese grater)

Mix both ingredients together and sprinkle over hot, cooked vegetables. Makes enough for $1/2$ pound cooked vegetables.

Familia (Dry Cereal)

This recipe comes from Del Karabensh, wife of Jerry, who has served as a member of the Jews for Jesus Board of Directors. Del says that she stores the unused portion in her freezer because she grinds her grains fresh, and freezing preserves the vitamins.

1   box (2 pounds, 10 ounces) quick oats, or 12 cups rolled oats
2   cups bran (wheat or oat)
2   cups raisins
2   cups ground or milled grain—wheat, millet, barley, soy, etc.
3   cups almonds, chopped
3   cups sesame seeds or raw sunflower seeds
3   cups unsweetened coconut

Process bran and raisins together, $1/2$ cup at a time, in food processor until chopped. Mix all ingredients together and keep in large, covered container. Serve in small amounts ($1/4$-$1/2$ cup at time) in bowl with cold milk for breakfast. Let soak or eat immediately.

Garlic Butter for Garlic Bread

This recipe comes from Mary-Carol Larson, a Jews for Jesus friend. Spread mix on plain, sliced French or Italian bread. Wrap bread in aluminum foil and bake at 350° for 25 minutes.

1   stick ($1/2$ cup) butter, softened
$1/4$ cup Parmesan cheese, grated
1-2   cloves garlic, minced
2   tablespoons dried parsley flakes
$1/2$ teaspoon Italian seasoning

To softened butter cream in remaining ingredients, mix well, spread on bread. Follow above directions. Yields 1 loaf.

Cakes, Pies and Cookies:
What's Life Without a Little Nosh?

Jews for Jesus is a mobile ministry. We'll go anywhere, anytime to preach the Gospel to anyone who will listen. Our traveling music team, The Liberated Wailing Wall, carries the message of good news throughout the country with its Jewish Gospel music. As they travel, they naturally eat. In fact, they've developed a philosophy called "eating for history's sake." They always make sure to experience the local fare of the area in which they're ministering, for who knows if and when they'll ever be there again? In Brooklyn, New York the team has to go to Junior's Restaurant, which is famous for its cheesecake. When down South they have to eat all the pecan pie they're offered. And in California they feel they have to find the perfect carrot cake. That's eating for history's sake. We're glad they're not starving!

And speaking of eating for history's sake—most of us have an Aunt Martha or a Tanta Sophie who are famous for one particular type of pie or another. We know an Aunt Phyllis whose recipe for pumpkin pie is so delicious, we've put it in this cookbook. One of the Jews for Jesus volunteers, a co-laborer in Messiah, gave us her Aunt Rose's recipe for honey cake. And for the health-conscious, we've included Cindy Cole's recipe for a good-for-ya cookie.

One of the hazards in looking through this chapter is that you may find yourself becoming very hungry. Your stomach may surprise you by rumbling loudly. Even if it's the middle of the afternoon you may suddenly want to run out and buy the ingredients for Breakfast Cheese Pie, and bake one immediately. You may find yourself developing your own theory of eating for history's sake. Who knows when you'll find yourself in this particular place, at this particular time, ever again? And shouldn't you and your family have something to remember the moment by? It may sound silly, but it doesn't matter. Eat and drink unto the Lord, and make a joyful noise as you do.

We Wish You Could See this Recipe for Coffee Cake

This recipe was given to us by Karen Marks of Palatine, Illinois. She has the most beautiful handwriting. This recipe was hand-written in lovely, flourished letters, and the recipe is a joy to look at as well as to make and eat. The result is an unusual type of coffee cake with a surprise cheese filling.

Batter:
1	cup butter or margarine, softened
1	cup sugar
2	eggs
2	cups flour
2	teaspoons baking powder
1/2	teaspoon salt

Cream butter or margarine together with sugar. Add eggs and beat well. Sift flour with baking powder and salt; add to creamed mixture a little at a time. Batter will be very thick—the consistency of cookie dough.

Filling:
2	8-ounce packages cream cheese, softened
1	egg yolk
1/2	cup sugar
1	teaspoon vanilla extract

Cream all together well and set aside.

Topping:
1/4	cup sugar
1/2	cup flour
4	tablespoons (1/2 stick) butter or margarine

Combine sugar and flour and cut in butter or margarine until crumbly.

Spread half of the cake batter in a well-greased 9"x13" pan.* Pour filling over batter and follow with the rest of the batter (work carefully to spread batter evenly over the filling. You will probably find it impossible to completely seal the edges. Don't be concerned, as this will not affect the cake once it's baked). Follow with the topping and bake at 350° for 45-60 minutes, until tester inserted in center comes out clean. While still warm, drizzle a thin glaze of powdered sugar, milk and vanilla extract over top, if desired (the cake is so rich, you may not find the glaze necessary). Makes 12 servings.

*If you choose to bake this in a round Bundt or springform pan, divide the batter into thirds. After spreading first layer onto bottom of greased pan, pour on half of the filling. Then drop tablespoons of the batter onto the filling, working carefully to spread it evenly. Again, note that it will be impossible to seal the edges completely. Pour on remainder of filling and spread on the rest of batter. Follow with the topping mixture and bake as directed above. Drizzle glaze over top of cake after it's removed from the pan.

Delicious Surprise (or the Lazy Person's Chocolate Chipper)

One evening Janie-sue Wertheim's husband Steve had a sweet tooth attack. Janie-sue was feeling too lazy that night to do much about it. She didn't exactly want to bake cookies, but she knew Steve felt that he had to have something sweet and chewy. When she asked him what he wanted, he said, "Oh, I don't know, but make it delicious and make it a surprise." This is what she made.

1	cup butter or margarine, softened
1	cup sugar
1/2	cup brown sugar, packed
2	eggs
2	teaspoons vanilla
2 1/4	cups flour
1/2	teaspoon salt
1	teaspoon baking soda
1/2	cup raisins
1	12-ounce package chocolate chips (semisweet or milk chocolate)
1/2	cup walnuts, chopped
3/4	cup mini-marshmallows

Cream butter or margarine, sugars, eggs and vanilla in food processor or by hand. Slowly add a few marshmallows and process until almost smooth; repeat until all marshmallows are blended in (if working by hand mix in marshmallows as well as you can). Blend in the flour, salt and baking soda. Add raisins, chocolate chips and nuts by hand with wooden spoon. Spread batter evenly in a greased and floured 9"x13" pan. Bake at 350° approximately 45 minutes, or until done. Cut into squares when cool. Makes approximately 18 squares, depending upon how large or small you cut them.

Banana Cake in a Loaf

1	cup sugar
1	stick butter or margarine
2	eggs
1	teaspoon baking soda
4	tablespoons sour cream or plain yogurt
1	cup banana, mashed
1 1/2	cups flour
1	teaspoon vanilla

In large bowl, cream together sugar and butter or margarine; add eggs and beat all together well. Dissolve the baking soda in sour cream or yogurt; add to mixture. Add remaining ingredients and beat well. Bake in well-greased loaf pan at 375° for 45 minutes. Let cool in pan 5 minutes; turn out onto baking rack and let cool completely before slicing. Makes 10 servings.

Janet Regan's Apple Squares

Mrs. Regan is a friend of the Jews for Jesus, and she says that she created this recipe especially for her husband and six children. She usually omits the sugar because her husband is diabetic, and no one seems to notice that the sugar is missing. Janet assured us that when you roll out the crust, it isn't necessary for it to be a perfect rectangle. No matter how funny it looks going into the oven, it's always delicious when it comes out.

Crust:
3	cups plus 6 tablespoons flour
1½	teaspoons salt
1¼	sticks plus 1 tablespoon margarine
8	tablespoons ice water

Put flour and salt in large bowl. Cut in margarine until crumbly. Add ice water and mix well with a fork. Do not overhandle dough! Dampen a table or countertop and lay a piece of waxed paper a bit larger than a 9"x13" jelly roll pan over it. Divide dough in half. Roll out half the dough to fit pan. Transfer dough from the waxed paper to the pan.

Filling:
12	large cooking apples, peeled, cored and sliced thin
½	cup sugar
1½	teaspoons cinnamon
¼	teaspoon salt
	butter or margarine

Lay the apple slices over the first layer of dough in pan. Mix together sugar, cinnamon and salt and sprinkle evenly over apples. Dot with butter or margarine. Roll out top crust. Place over apples and crimp edges together with the tines of a fork. Bake 35 minutes at 375°. Cut into squares when cool. Makes 18 squares.

Note: If desired, before cutting into squares, you may glaze with 1 cup confectioner's sugar (sifted), a few drops of lemon extract and a few drops of milk mixed together to make a thin, spreadable glaze.

California Carrot Cake

This recipe was submitted by Ruth Esther Snyder, a Jews for Jesus missionary staff wife. Many people know her husband Avi for his dramatic portrayal of Saul of Tarsus, which he has presented in many churches. We think Ruth Esther is especially talented, too—she's been married to Avi for years! The Snyder's presently live with their family in the former Soviet Union, where Avi leads the Jews for Jesus work.

1	cup raisins
¾	cup honey
1	cup carrots, grated

2	tablespoons butter or margarine
1 1/2	cups water
1	teaspoon cinnamon
1	teaspoon ground allspice
1	teaspoon salt
1/2	teaspoon nutmeg
1/4	teaspoon ground cloves

Mix all of the above in a medium saucepan. Bring to a boil over medium heat; lower heat and simmer for 20 minutes. When cool, add the following:

1 1/2	cups whole wheat flour
1/2	cup wheat germ
1	teaspoon baking soda

Pour batter into greased 9"x5" loaf pan and bake at 325° for 1 hour or until cake tester inserted in center comes out clean. Makes 1 loaf.

Note: 1/2 cup chopped nuts (walnuts or pecans) can be added along with the dry ingredients. Also, 1 cup grated zucchini (unpeeled) can replace the carrots for a delicious zucchini loaf.

Danish Kringle ala Mrs. Starks

Mrs. Starks of Toledo, Ohio says that you must try this recipe to see just how good pastry can be even when it's made without sugar.

4	cups flour
3	sticks margarine or butter
3/4	cup evaporated milk
1/4	cup water
1	egg

Mix all as for pie crust until crumbly. Put on lightly floured board and cut into four pieces. Roll out each piece into a 12"x16" rectangle. Spoon in filling (recipe follows). Lap each side over filling, long edges meeting in the middle. Pinch ends together. Bake at 350° for 35-40 minutes. Makes 4 pastry rolls.

Filling:

2	(21-ounce) cans fruit, packed in its own juice (peaches are especially good)
3	tablespoons cornstarch

Cook together until thickened. Let cool before filling pastry.

Mum's English Currant Cake

Angi Silverstein's grandmother, Bubby Ida, came from a little shtetl (town) in Poland, and there she learned to be a great cook. When Angi's mother (a nice Gentile girl from England), married Ida's son, she determined to become an authentic Jewish cook. Armed with Bubby Ida's recipes and a great deal of determination, she took on the task. First she made potato pancakes, which turned out perfectly, except that she served them with pork chops! Next, she tried to make dumplings, called kreplach, but when she placed them in chicken soup they disintegrated into shreds.

Eventually Angi's mother came to a decision. She would leave the Jewish cooking to Bubby Ida and concentrate on what she knew best: English cooking. Here are two of her favorites.

6	ounces currants
4	ounces margarine
4	ounces sugar
8	ounces self-rising flour
2	tablespoons orange marmalade
1	egg
2	ounces milk

Mix first 4 ingredients together.
Dough should look like fine bread crumbs.
Stir together milk, egg and marmalade and add to dough.
Blend all ingredients together well.
Place in well-greased round 6" cake tin with high sides. Bake 1 hour at 375°.
Makes 6 servings.

Easy Cornish Pasties

1	(8-ounce) can corned beef
1	medium onion, diced
1	large potato, boiled and diced
1	egg, beaten
1	tablespoon dry onion soup mix
1	package pie crust mix
	milk

Mix together the first 5 ingredients in a medium bowl.
Prepare crust according to package directions and divide into 4 equal portions.
Roll out each portion on a floured board into circles approximately 8" in diameter.
Spoon 1/4 of the meat mixture on each pastry circle.
Fold circle over and press to seal edges. Brush top with a little milk.
Bake on cookie sheet for 45 minutes at 375°.
Makes 4 servings.

Baklava (a Middle Eastern Specialty)

If you've ever eaten in a Middle Eastern restaurant, be it Greek, Persian, Israeli or Arabic, you may have seen baklava on the dessert menu. At one time it was unthinkable for the average American to try making this delicacy, as it requires a special, extremely thin dough called phyllo. Perhaps there are still some patient cooks out there who make their own phyllo leaves. We do not happen to know anyone like this, but we do know packaged phyllo can be found in most supermarkets these days. We thank Marion Shacklett from Tulsa for this unthinkably good recipe.

1	pound walnuts, finely ground
1/2	cup sugar
2	teaspoons cinnamon
1/8	teaspoon ground cloves
1/4	cup finely ground fresh bread crumbs
1	pound phyllo leaves, defrosted according to package instructions
1	pound sweet, unsalted butter, melted (with foam skimmed off top)

Syrup:

2	cups sugar
1	cup honey
2	cups water
1	teaspoon cinnamon
2	whole cloves
1	teaspoon lemon juice

In small bowl, combine walnuts, sugar, cinnamon, cloves and bread crumbs.
Brush 12"x17"x1" baking sheet with melted butter.
Place 6 phyllo leaves on bottom, brushing each 1 with melted butter as you go.
Spread 1/2 cup walnut mixture over these layers.
Repeat with remaining leaves and nut mixture, reserving about 6 leaves for the top.
Brush top with remaining melted butter.
With a sharp, pointed knife, score the top sheets in small diamond or square shapes.
Bake in 350° oven for 35-45 minutes, until golden brown but not burnt around the edges.
Let cool completely.
Heat together syrup ingredients in medium saucepan until warm and well-blended.
Remove the cloves and pour warm syrup evenly over top of baklava.
Allow to cool for one day before eating.
Makes 20-25 servings, depending upon how you cut the layers.

Note: Phyllo leaves can be tricky to work with—they dry out quickly if left uncovered. After defrosting leaves, unroll on clean dishtowel and cover with another clean towel. Keep leaves covered as you work, and try to work quickly.

Viv's Baklava Rolls

2 $\frac{1}{2}$ cups sugar
2 cups water
$\frac{1}{4}$ cup honey
juice of $\frac{1}{2}$ orange or 1 teaspoon orange extract
1 pound phyllo leaves
$\frac{1}{2}$ pound sweet, unsalted butter, melted
5 cups walnuts, chopped
2 $\frac{1}{2}$ teaspoons ground cinnamon
1 teaspoon ground cloves

Boil together sugar, water and honey until slightly thickened over medium heat; add orange juice or extract and let cool. Take two sheets phyllo dough and place in greased jelly roll pan or cookie sheet. Brush lightly with melted butter. Mix together chopped walnuts and spices. Spread $\frac{1}{2}$ cup nut mixture at one end of dough; turn in long ends and roll gently. Place, ends down in pan. Repeat with remaining sheets (double the sheets) until nut mixture is used up. Refrigerate, then slice diagonally into $1\frac{1}{2}$"-2" pieces. Bake at 325° for 25 minutes. Makes 20 servings.

Home on the Ranch Carrot Cake

If you're familiar with Jews for Jesus history, you might recognize the name Ann Ward. Ann and her husband Mike were the proprietors of The Ranch in Coos Bay, Oregon where a few of the first Jews for Jesus found the Lord. The Ward's felt called by God at that time to open their farm to those whom the Lord would send them. In those days, a rather motley-looking group visited them, accepted the Lord and later became the first Jews for Jesus missionaries. Mike and Ann were faithful to the Lord, even when it meant entertaining a rather uncertain-looking group of hippies!

We are thankful for Ann and Mike. Here's her recipe for carrot cake, which fed many new Jews for Jesus.

3 cups grated carrots
3 cups flour
2 cups sugar
2 teaspoons baking soda
1 teaspoon salt
1 teaspoon cinnamon

Put the above ingredients in a large mixing bowl; stir well. Make a well in the center of the ingredients. Add:

1 $\frac{1}{2}$ cups vegetable oil
2 eggs, beaten
1 teaspoon vanilla
1 cup dates, pitted and chopped
1 cup walnuts, chopped

Mix together well with dry ingredients. Pour into a greased 9"x13" or tube pan and bake at 350° for 40 minutes. Frost when cool.

Frosting:

4	cups confectioner's sugar, sifted
8	ounces cream cheese, softened
1/2	teaspoon orange extract (or almond or vanilla)
1	tablespoon malt powder, plain (optional)
	pinch salt

Mix well and spread on cooled cake. Makes 12 servings.

Mint Squares Fit for a Wedding

There are many things we Jews for Jesus love about our work—handing out Gospel broadsides, talking to people about Y'shua, singing our Jewish gospel music—and attending Jewish weddings. Martha Ruth Jacobs, a third-generation Jewish Christian, was a missionary with the New York branch of Jews for Jesus before she and her husband Loren felt called to open a Messianic ministry in Detroit, Michigan. Martha has often been asked to prepare this recipe for chocolate mint squares for Jews for Jesus weddings. This recipe brings rave reviews each and every time.

Bottom layer:

2	eggs, beaten
1/2	cup butter, melted
2	squares unsweetened chocolate, melted
1	cup sugar
1/2	teaspoon vanilla extract
1/2	cup flour

Combine all ingredients, except flour, and beat well. Add in flour and mix until smooth. Pour into greased 9" square pan. Bake at 350° for 25 minutes.

Frosting:

2	tablespoons butter, softened
1	tablespoon heavy cream
1	cup confectioner's sugar, sifted
1/2	teaspoon peppermint extract
	few drops green food coloring

Mix all ingredients together well. Spread over cooled bottom layer. When frosting is firm, spread on topping.

Topping:

1	square unsweetened chocolate, melted
1	tablespoon butter or margarine, melted

Mix together, and spread over frosting. Place in refrigerator until firm. Cut into small squares. Makes 25 servings.

Eat Your Cereal Cake (Semolina Cake)

This cake is made with a familiar childhood cereal, cream of wheat, yet once it is baked, it's hard to tell that it's a main ingredient. It is a Tunisian recipe, very unusual, very simple to make and very good. Our thanks to an Israeli friend, Daphna, who gave us this recipe and fed it to some of our more fortunate staff members.

3 1/4   cups semolina (cream of wheat cereal)
1 3/4   cups sugar
2   tablespoons crushed almonds
1/4   cup oil
2   eggs
1/2   cup water
1   teaspoon almond extract
1   teaspoon rum extract

Syrup:
3/4   cup sugar
1   cup water
2-3   tablespoons lemon juice

Mix all ingredients for cake together in a large bowl, stirring very well. Grease well a 9"x13' baking pan, and pour batter into it. Bake cake at 350° for 35 minutes. Prepare syrup by bringing ingredients to a boil in a medium saucepan; lower heat and cook for 25 minutes, stirring occasionally. When cake is baked, pour syrup over top. Cut cake on diagonal into diamond-shaped pieces. Makes 12-18 servings.

Italian Pound Cake

This recipe was given to us by Anna Maria Hasch, of Anna's Soup Kitchen fame.

6   eggs
2   cups sugar
1   cup oil
1   teaspoon vanilla
4   cups flour
3   teaspoons baking powder
1   teaspoon baking soda
1/2   teaspoon salt
1/2   cup milk
1/2   cup orange juice (or pineapple juice)

Beat eggs well in a bowl. Add sugar, oil and vanilla; beat until thick. Add flour, baking powder, soda and salt (sifted together) alternately with milk and juice. Beat well. Pour into greased Bundt pan and bake at 350° for 1 hour, or in a 9"x13" pan for 40-45 minutes. Makes 12 servings.

Chocolate Bar Swirl Cake

1	cup margarine or butter
2	cups sugar
1	teaspoon vanilla
5	eggs
2 ½	cups flour
¾	teaspoon baking soda
¼	teaspoon salt
1 ½	cup sour cream
¼	cup honey
¾	cup chopped pecans
1	milk chocolate bar (½ pound)
½	cup chocolate syrup

Cream butter or margarine with sugar and vanilla until light and fluffy; add eggs and beat well. Combine flour, baking soda and salt; add alternately with sour cream to creamed butter mixture. Stir honey and pecans into 2 cups of the batter; set aside. Melt chocolate bar in chocolate syrup over warm water; blend into remaining batter. Pour into a greased and floured 10" tube pan. Spoon reserved mixture evenly over chocolate batter. Bake on lowest rack of oven at 350° for 45 minutes; decrease to 325° for 50-55 minutes. Cool in pan 1 hour. Turn out onto cake rack and continue cooling. Makes 10-12 servings

Easy-Breezy Apple Cake

The ease of this recipe from Janie-Sue Wertheim is that the top of the cake gets crusty as it bakes, eliminating the need for frosting.

4	eggs
2	cups sugar
1	cup oil
2	cups flour
4	teaspoons baking powder
4	teaspoons cinnamon
½	teaspoon salt
2	teaspoons vanilla extract
4	apples, peeled and chopped

Beat eggs well in large bowl.
Add sugar and oil. Sift together dry ingredients and add to egg mixture.
Stir in extract and chopped apples.
Pour into greased 13"x9" pan and bake at 350° for 45-60 minutes, or until done.
Makes 12 servings.

Apple Cake

3	eggs
1 1/4	cup vegetable oil
1 3/4	cup sugar
3	cups flour, sifted
2	teaspoons baking soda
2	teaspoons vanilla
3/4	teaspoon salt
3	cups apples, diced
1	cup walnuts, chopped
1/2	teaspoon cinnamon

Mix well together eggs, oil and sugar.
Sift together flour and baking soda; add to egg mixture.
Add vanilla and salt; blend well.
Stir in apples, walnuts and cinnamon.
Pour into a greased and floured 9"x13" pan; bake at 350° for 35-40 minutes.
Delicious served warm with ice cream or whipped cream.
Makes 12 servings.

Cecilia's Creation Cake

This is a famous Cecilia Butcher creation, which she often has on hand for starving Jews for Jesus missionaries as they wander in and out of her house.

1	package two-layer yellow cake mix
	(use the cheapest one you can find)
3/4	cup white wine
3/4	cup oil
1	teaspoon nutmeg
4	eggs
	confectioner's sugar for dusting

Mix together all ingredients except confectioner's sugar,
beating with electric mixer for 5 minutes until well blended.
Pour into greased and floured Bundt pan.
Bake at 350° for 45 minutes or until toothpick inserted in center comes out clean.
Cool for 15 minutes on wire rack; remove from Bundt pan and place on cake plate to complete cooling.
Dust with confectioner's sugar.
Makes 12 servings.

Rhubarb Cake

This recipe comes from Jo Ellen Mass, an old Seattle friend of Diane Cohen.

2	cups flour
1	teaspoon baking soda
1/8	teaspoon salt
1 1/2	cups sugar
1/2	cup margarine
1	teaspoon vanilla
1	egg, beaten
1	cup regular sour cream or fat-free substitute
2	cups fresh rhubarb, chopped
1/2	cup brown sugar
1/4	cup white sugar
1-2	tablespoons butter or margarine.

Sift together flour, baking soda and salt. Cream together margarine and sugar; add vanilla and egg. Alternately add flour mixture to margarine mixture with 1 cup sour cream. Mix well, then stir in chopped rhubarb. Pour batter into greased and floured 7 1/2"x11 1/2" pan. Make streusel of brown sugar, white sugar and margarine or butter; sprinkle over batter. Bake at 375° for 30 minutes. Makes 10 servings.

Fantastic Cake

1/2	cup (1 stick) butter or margarine
1	cup flour
1	cup pecans, chopped
8	ounces cream cheese
1	cup powdered sugar
1	cup non-dairy whipped topping
2	(3 1/2 ounces each) packages instant chocolate pudding mix
3	cups milk
	chopped pecans for garnish
	non-dairy whipped topping for garnish

Melt butter or margarine.

Mix with flour and pecans; press dough into 9"x13" pan and bake at 375° for 15 minutes.

Let cool.

Mix together cream cheese with powdered sugar; fold in non-dairy topping.

Spread mixture over cooled crust; chill.

Mix chocolate pudding with milk; spread over cake in pan and chill.

Garnish with whipped topping and more chopped pecans.

Chill 2 hours.

Makes 12 servings.

Aunt Minnie's Apple Cake

Yael Neffinger catered her own wedding and rehearsal dinner. Born in Israel, she married a handsome architect named Greg and together they settled in Massachusetts. Yael is an expert at cooking large quantities of food, for which she usually wears an apron and not a wedding dress. Her Aunt Minnie lent us this recipe.

3	tablespoons sesame seeds
1 1/2	cups vegetable oil
2	cups brown sugar OR 1 1/4 cups honey
3	eggs
3	cups flour, sifted
1	teaspoon baking soda
1	teaspoon baking powder
1/2	teaspoon ground cardamom
1	teaspoon ground cinnamon
2	teaspoons vanilla extract
3	tablespoons apple juice, milk or water
3	cups apples, chopped (do not need to be peeled— can be chopped fine in food processor)
1	cup chopped pecans, walnuts or almonds

Preheat oven to 350°. Grease a 10" Bundt pan, two 9" round cake pans or one 9"x13" pan. Sprinkle the bottom and sides with sesame seeds. Beat the oil and sugar or honey in large bowl until creamy. Add eggs, one at a time, beating well after each addition. In separate bowl, sift together flour, baking powder, baking soda and spices. Add the dry ingredients and vanilla to the egg mixture, along with whatever liquid you choose, beating until batter is smooth. Fold in the chopped apples and nuts. Pour batter into pan and bake for 30-45 minutes, depending upon size of pan, until knife inserted in center comes out clean (if using honey, cake will need 1 1/4 hours to bake). Remove from oven and cool. Makes 10 servings.

Jewish Kringler

1	cup flour
1/2	cup butter
1	tablespoon water

Mix together like pie crust. Pat along the sides of a cookie sheet in 2 long strips, each 3" wide.

1	cup water
1/2	cup butter
1	cup flour
3	eggs
1/2	teaspoon vanilla extract

Put water and butter in saucepan; heat to boiling over medium heat. Remove pan from heat; add flour all at once and stir until smooth. Stir in eggs, one at a time, and beat well with a wooden spoon after each addition. Add vanilla. Spread over strips of dough mixture in cookie sheet, making sure dough is completely covered. Bake at 350° for 1 hour. When cool frost with:

$1^1/_2$ cup confectioner's sugar
$1^1/_2$ tablespoons butter, softened
  $^1/_2$ teaspoon almond or vanilla extract
       heavy cream

Mix sugar, butter and extract together with enough heavy cream to make a spreadable frosting. Makes 10-12 servings.

Fruity Lowfat Cheesecake

  1   cup All-Bran cereal (reduced to crumbs in food processor or blender)
$^1/_4$ cup diet or light margarine, melted
  2   (15-ounce) containers light ricotta cheese
$^1/_2$ cup liquid nondairy creamer
$^1/_2$ cup sugar
  2   tablespoons flour
  1   tablespoon lemon juice (fresh, if possible)
  1   teaspoon each grated fresh lemon and orange peel
$^1/_4$ teaspoon salt
  2   eggs (or 3 egg whites)
      fresh fruit, sliced

Prepare crust by mixing together crushed cereal and melted margarine; press into bottom and sides of 8" or 9" springform pan (if springform pan is not available, use round Pyrex or corning ware dish). Put crust in refrigerator. In large bowl add all remaining ingredients, except eggs and fruit. Beat well with electric mixer until smooth. Add eggs (or whites), one at a time, until smooth. Pour batter over crust. Bake in preheated 350° oven for 60 minutes or until center is firm. Shut off oven. Cool in oven with door slightly ajar for 30 minutes. Chill 3 hours in refrigerator and top with fresh sliced fruit (kiwi and strawberries are nice). Makes 10 servings.

Breakfast (or Anytime) Cheese Pie

Beverly Gibbs of Flagstaff, Arizona gave us this recipe. It's an excellent dish for brunch or anytime a protein-rich dessert is needed to balance out a meal. The Moskowitz's traditionally have this pie for Christmas breakfast at our home.

1	(8-ounce) can refrigerated crescent rolls
3	tablespoons butter or margarine
1/4	cup sugar
2	eggs
15	ounces (2 cups) ricotta cheese
1/4	teaspoon vanilla or almond extract
1/4	cup golden raisins

Streusel topping:
1/2	cup flour
1/4	cup brown sugar
1/4	teaspoon cinnamon
1/4	cup butter or margarine, softened

Separate crescent rolls into triangles. Place 2 triangles of dough in 10" pie pan so that their bases meet in the center and the pointed ends drape over opposite sides. Place 2 more triangles at right angles to the first pieces. The center of their base should meet the first pieces at the seam, and pointed ends should drape over pan edges. The dough will look like a star. Fit remaining triangles of dough over pan sides and bottom, letting pointed tips drape over sides. Press edges together to seal. Beat together filling ingredients until well blended. Pour into dough-lined pan. Mix together ingredients for streusel topping. Drop topping in small bits over cheese filling. Fold pointed tips of dough over filling. Bake at 350° for 35-40 minutes; let cool. Makes 6 servings.

Last-Minute Sour Cream Pie

This recipe is one of the easiest, most successful desserts you'll ever make. It is especially good for those times when you have company coming and you're too busy to make an extravagant dessert.

1	8-inch graham cracker crust, store-bought
1	cup sour cream
1	cup milk
1	(3 1/2-ounce) package instant pudding*

Beat sour cream with milk until smooth. Blend in pudding mix until smooth and slightly thickened. Pour into graham cracker crust and chill 1 hour or until set. If desired, serve with whipped cream. Makes 6 servings.

*vanilla (for the basic recipe) or butterscotch pudding
banana pudding—add sliced bananas on top of pie
chocolate pudding—garnish top with chocolate shavings

The Chocolate Lover's Revenge Pie

2	squares unsweetened chocolate
1	stick (1/2 cup) butter or margarine
1/4	cup flour, sifted
2	eggs
1	cup sugar

Melt butter or margarine with chocolate in top of double boiler over hot, but not boiling, water. Mix flour and sugar together in bowl; beat eggs and combine with flour/sugar mixture. Add chocolate mixture. Pour into well-greased 9" pie tin and bake at 350° for 30-45 minutes or until set. Serve with whipped topping or ice cream when cool. Makes 6-8 servings.

November '77 Squash Pie

The only clue as to the history of this dessert is that it was scribbled on a date book page for November 9, 1977. But there's nothing mysterious about its taste.

Cornmeal pastry:

1	cup flour
1/2	cup yellow cornmeal
1/2	teaspoon salt
1/2	cup shortening
1/4	cup water

Combine flour, cornmeal and salt in a bowl. Cut in shortening with a fork or pastry blender until mixture resembles coarse meal. Sprinkle with water and stir with a fork. Pat into a ball and put on a lightly floured board. Roll out and fit gently into a 9" pie plate.

Pumpkin or squash filling:

2	cups canned pumpkin (not pumpkin pie mix) or strained, cooked butternut or acorn squash
1	cup brown sugar
1	cup heavy cream
1	cup milk
6	eggs, lightly beaten
1/2	cup crystallized ginger, finely chopped
2	teaspoons cinnamon
1/4	teaspoon ground cloves
1/4	teaspoon salt
1	teaspoon brandy-flavored extract

Mix all the filling ingredients together in large bowl until well blended. Pour into pie shell. Bake at 350° for 45 minutes or until the filling is set around the edges but still a bit runny in the center. Cool completely before eating. Makes 6-8 servings.

Coconut Pie

1	piecrust, ready-made
1/2	cup unsalted butter
1 1/2	cups sugar
3	eggs, beaten
4	teaspoons fresh lemon juice
1	teaspoon vanilla extract
1 1/2	cups unsweetened shredded coconut

Preheat oven to 450°. Bake crust until golden, about 8 minutes. Cool. Reduce oven temperature to 350°. Melt butter over low heat. Add sugar and stir until mixture is heated through. Add eggs, lemon juice and vanilla, and whisk to combine. Stir in the coconut. Pour filling into prepared crust. Bake for 40 minutes or until filling is deep golden brown. Remove from oven and let cool slightly, refrigerate, covered, until completely cool. Before serving, garnish with shredded coconut, if desired. Makes 8 servings.

Aunt Phyllis' Pumpkin Pie

Hats off to Phyllis Grull, of Denver, Colorado, who gave us the recipe for this pie. Actually, the recipe comes from Mr. Grull's Aunt Emma, who gave it to the Grulls at their wedding reception, along with this poem:

> *What moistens the lips*
> *What brightens the eye*
> *What calls back the past*
> *Like a rich pumpkin pie?*

2	eggs
1	scant cup sugar
1	tablespoon flour
1	cup canned or cooked pumpkin (not pumpkin pie mix)
1	cup half-and-half
1	teaspoon cinnamon
1/4	teaspoon ginger
1/4	teaspoon nutmeg
1	unbaked 9" pie shell

Mix all ingredients together and pour into unbaked pie shell.
Bake at 400° for 30 minutes; turn oven down to 350° for 15 minutes more.
Let cool.
Makes 6-8 servings.

Easy Pie Crust

1 1/2   cups flour
1   teaspoon salt
1 1/2   teaspoons sugar
1/2   cup oil
2   tablespoons cold milk

Sift dry ingredients into a pie plate; add oil and milk and mix with fork until evenly dampened. Press crust up sides and along the bottom of the pie pan. Bake at 425° for 12-15 minutes. Check often because it burns easily. Makes 1 crust.

Vinegar Pie Pastry

4   cups flour
1   tablespoon sugar
2   teaspoons salt
1 3/4   cups shortening (Crisco)
1/2   cup water
2   tablespoons cider vinegar
1   egg

Combine flour, sugar and salt with a pastry blender and cut in shortening until mixture resembles coarse crumbs. Combine water, vinegar and egg and beat with fork—pour into flour mixture; mix well until pastry holds together (dough will be sticky). Cover and chill at least 2 hours. Divide into 4 or 5 balls; wrap each tightly with plastic wrap and refrigerate. Will keep in refrigerator up to 2 weeks. Makes 4-5 single pie crusts.

Boston Cookies

1   cup butter or margarine
1 1/2   cups sugar
3   eggs
1   teaspoon baking soda
1 1/2   tablespoons hot water
3 1/4   cups flour
1/2   teaspoon salt
1   teaspoon cinnamon
1   cup chopped walnuts
3/4   cup currants or raisins

Cream butter or margarine, add sugar gradually and beat in eggs one at a time. Dissolve baking soda in hot water. Sift flour together with salt and cinnamon. Add half of flour mixture to butter mixture, stirring well. Stir in baking soda mixture; add rest of flour mixture and walnuts and currants or raisins. Blend well. Drop by rounded teaspoonfuls onto greased cookie sheet, about 1" inch apart. Bake at 350° until lightly browned. Makes 3-4 dozen.

Healthy Bran Brownies

Maybe the words healthy bran are incongruous with brownies, but Diane Cohen assures us these are delicious and perfect for chocoholics who are watching their cholesterol. Diane says these are perfectly fudgy and gooey.

- 3 tablespoons unsweetened cocoa
- 1 tablespoon instant coffee
- 1 tablespoon water
- 2 ripe bananas, mashed
- 2 cups sugar
- 6 egg whites
- 1 teaspoon vanilla
- 1 cup oat bran
- 1/4 teaspoon salt
- 1 cup walnuts, chopped or 1 cup raisins

Combine cocoa, coffee, water and bananas in blender or blend with hand mixer.

Add remaining ingredients and mix all together well.

Pour into 9" greased baking pan (sprayed with cooking spray) and bake at 350° for 45 minutes.

Makes 12 servings.

Chocolate Scotcheroos

Winona Wellsfry submitted this recipe, admitting that whenever she's on a diet she dreams about eating sweets.

- 1 cup sugar
- 1 cup light corn syrup
- 1 cup peanut butter
- 6 cups crispy rice cereal
- 1 cup semisweet chocolate chips
- 1 cup butterscotch chips

Cook sugar and corn syrup together in a heavy medium saucepan over medium high heat until mixture boils (watch carefully).

Remove from heat and stir in peanut butter, blending well.

Add rice cereal and stir until well mixed.

Press into 9"x13" pan.

Over low heat, in small saucepan, melt both types of chips, stirring frequently with wooden spoon.

When melted, spread over cereal mixture.

Chill until firm, cut into bars.

Makes 16 servings.

Traditional Jewish Rugelach

Don't worry about how to pronounce rugelach. These are the cookies that we Jews for Jesus dream about. We need them like a hole in the head (they're made with a pound of butter), but we love them anyway because they remind us of our youth. If we ever visit you at your house, and you serve us these little cakes, we will be forever indebted to you.

1	pound sweet, unsalted butter
8	ounces cream cheese (can be the low-fat variety)
3 1/2	cups flour
3	tablespoons sour cream (can also be reduced-fat)
1/4	cup sugar
	pinch salt
16	ounces apricot or strawberry jam, or marmalade
1/2	cup walnuts, finely chopped

Cream together butter and cream cheese. Add flour, sour cream, sugar and salt. Knead well to form a stiff dough. Refrigerate for several hours until firm. Roll into 9" circles, using about 1/6 of the dough for each circle. Combine jam or marmalade with chopped walnuts and spread on each circle. Cut each circle into 8 wedge-shaped sections. Roll each wedge, starting from the large end and ending with the point. Curve to form a crescent, placing open end down on a buttered baking sheet. Bake at 375° for 15 minutes or until browned. Makes 4 dozen.

Good For Ya Cookies

Cindy Cole of Lancaster, California sent us this recipe for healthy, delicious cookies. You might try substituting part white or whole wheat pastry flour for some of the whole wheat flour, to make a lighter cookie.

1	cup butter or margarine
1/2	cup peanut butter
1	cup brown sugar
2	eggs
2	cups whole wheat flour
2	cups uncooked quick oatmeal
1	cup wheat germ
1	cup honey
1	cup raisins
1	cup flaked coconut
1/2	cup peanuts

Cream together first three ingredients; add eggs, beating well after each addition. Beat in flour, oatmeal and wheat germ with honey. Stir in raisins, coconut and peanuts. Drop by heaping teaspoonfuls onto greased cookie sheet. Bake at 375° for 10 minutes. Cool on wire rack. Makes 3 dozen.

Ethel's Sugar Cookies

$3/4$ cup butter or margarine (or a mixture of both)
1   cup sugar
2   eggs
$1/2$ teaspoon lemon or vanilla extract
2 $1/2$ cups flour
1   teaspoon baking powder
1   teaspoon salt

Cream together butter or margarine and sugar; add eggs and extract and blend thoroughly.
In separate bowl, stir together flour, baking powder and salt; blend into butter mixture.
Chill dough at least 1 hour.
Heat oven to 400°.
Roll dough out $1/8$" thick on lightly floured board.
Cut into shapes with cookie cutters.
Place on ungreased baking sheet.
Bake 6-8 minutes, or until cookies are a delicate golden color.
Makes about 4 dozen cookies.

Mary's Sugar Cookies

1 $1/2$ cups confectioner's sugar, sifted
1   cup butter or margarine
1   egg
1   teaspoon vanilla extract
$1/2$ teaspoon almond extract
2 $1/2$ cups flour
1   teaspoon baking soda
1   teaspoon cream of tartar
   sugar for sprinkling

Cream together confectioner's sugar with butter or margarine.
Mix in egg and extracts; blend thoroughly. In separate bowl, stir together dry ingredients; blend into sugar mixture.
Refrigerate dough for 2-3 hours. Heat oven to 375°.
Divide dough in half and roll 3/16" thick on lightly floured pastry cloth.
Cut with cookie cutters; sprinkle with sugar.
Place on lightly greased baking sheet.
Bake 7-8 minutes or until delicately golden.
Makes 5 dozen cookies.

Gingerbread Boys

Cheryl Rice, Jews for Jesus missionary, wife and mother of two, manages to find time for so many things because she knows where everything is in her house!

1/2	cup shortening
1/2	cup sugar
1/2	cup dark molasses
1/4	cup water
2 1/2	cups flour
3/4	teaspoon salt
1/2	teaspoon baking soda
3/4	teaspoon ginger
1/4	teaspoon nutmeg
1/8	teaspoon allspice
	raisins, candied cherries or red gumdrops, citron, string licorice, colored decorating icing— for decorating gingerbread boys

Cream together shortening and sugar. Blend in molasses, water, flour, salt, baking soda and spices. Cover bowl; chill 2-3 hours. Heat oven to 375°. Roll out dough 1/4" thick on lightly floured cloth-covered board. Cut with gingerbread boy (or girl) cutter; place on ungreased baking sheet. Press raisins into dough for eyes, nose and buttons. Use bits of candied cherries and strips of citron and string licorice for other trims. Bake 10-12 minutes. Remove immediately from baking sheet. Cool on wire rack. Trim with decorating icing (optional). Makes about fifteen 4" cookies.

Note: For crisper cookies, roll dough 1/8" thick. Bake 8 minutes. Makes about 2 dozen cookies.

Lekkas' Greek Cookies

One of the joys of having children is getting to know their friends, especially those who come from different ethnic backgrounds. Jessie has a Greek friend named Kassondra, and her mother Angie gave us this recipe.

1/2	pound unsalted butter, softened
2	pounds cake flour
2	egg yolks
4	tablespoons confectioners' sugar + extra for sprinkling
1/2	teaspoon baking soda
1/2	teaspoon baking powder
1	cup almonds, chopped fine
1	teaspoon anise extract
1	teaspoon vanilla extract

Blend butter and sugar together with electric beater in large mixing bowl at low speed for 10 minutes, or until smooth and very light. Add egg yolks, anise and vanilla extracts and continue beating. Add flour, baking soda and baking powder and mix until just blended. Stir in almonds with wooden spoon. Form dough into balls (a little smaller than walnuts) and place on ungreased baking sheet. Bake in preheated 350° oven for 10 minutes. Remove from cookie sheet and place on cooling rack. Before they cool, dust cookies with sifted confectioners' sugar. Makes 5 dozen.

Authentic Almond Cookies

Lori McHugh writes: "I checked this recipe with my local Chinese food store owner and he assured me that this recipe accurately duplicated authentic Chinese almond cookies, minus the lard."

1	cup shortening (like Crisco)
1	cup sugar
1/4	teaspoon almond extract
3	cups sifted all-purpose flour
36	whole, unblanched almonds
1	egg yolk
2	tablespoons water
	few drops yellow food coloring

Cream shortening together with sugar until fluffy, then blend in almond extract. Mix in flour 1 cup at a time, blending well after each addition. The mixture should be crumbly. Add a few drops of yellow food coloring to achieve a light yellow color.

Measure 1 level tablespoon of the dough and press with your hands to form a flat, round cookie 1 3/4" in diameter. Place on greased cookie sheet. Repeat with remaining dough, placing cookies 2" apart. Gently press an almond in the center of each cookie. Beat the egg yolk with water and brush lightly over cookie tops. Bake in 275° oven for 30 minutes; increase heat to 350° and bake for 10 minutes more or until lightly browned. Carefully remove to wire racks and cool (cookies will be very fragile when hot). Makes 3 dozen.

Brownies for Late-Night Cravings

Rumor has it that a certain member of the Jews for Jesus staff often experiences late-night cravings for chocolate, which must be satisfied immediately. This recipe for chocolate brownies comes from Ellen Zaretsky (who is not the mysterious chocolate-craver) and is recommended for cravings that strike any time of the day.

1	stick (1/2 cup) butter or margarine, melted
1	cup sugar
1	large or 2 small eggs
1/4	cup baking cocoa
1/4	teaspoon salt
3/4	cup all-purpose flour, sifted
1	teaspoon vanilla
1/2	cup chopped walnuts

Mix melted butter or margarine, sugar and eggs together in large bowl. Add cocoa, salt, flour, vanilla and walnuts mix well. Bake in greased 9"x9" pan at 350° for 30 minutes. Makes 12 servings.

Note: These are really chewy if cooked slightly underdone.

Authentic Scottish Shortbread

This recipe comes from the bed-and-breakfast establishment of Irene Sharpe in Troon, Scotland. It was written on the back of a receipt for a night's lodging.

9	ounces self-rising flour
3	ounces cornstarch
4	ounces superfine sugar
8	ounces sweet, unsalted butter

Mix flour, cornstarch and sugar in a medium bowl. Melt butter slowly over low flame. DO NOT LET IT BROWN. Add melted butter to dry ingredients and mix together well. Flatten dough into an ungreased 11"x7" pan. Bake at 350° for 30-45 minutes, until very lightly browned (almost blonde in color). Score with knife into diamond shapes; let cool. Makes 16 servings.

Lois' Pfefferneusse

Lois Link provided us with an education about *pfefferneusse* (German for "pepper nuts"). What we find in the common grocery store are cookies about the size of a walnut, on the soft side and rolled in powdered sugar. But they are not authentic *pfefferneusse*! Lois' friend, Gertrude Knodel Walz Johnson, who turned 80 years old in 1985, helped Lois understand what the cookies ought to be. Gertrude and her friends, during their childhood, used them as poker chips when their parents weren't looking! The dough is supposed to age a bit, and should be allowed to become as hard as a corn nut. This way, you can float the cookies in your coffee and dig them out with a spoon. The finished size of the cookies should be only a little bigger than a corn nut.

2	eggs
1	cup margarine
1	cup brown sugar
1	cup white sugar
2	teaspoons ground cinnamon
1/4	teaspoon nutmeg
1	teaspoon ground cloves
1	teaspoon ginger
1/2	teaspoon ground allspice
1	teaspoon salt
1	teaspoon pepper
1 1/2	teaspoons baking soda
1/2	teaspoon ground cardamon
1 1/3	cups dark molasses
4-5	cups flour

Cream together eggs, margarine and sugars. Add all the spices and the baking soda until well blended. Add molasses; stir in flour, cup by cup, to form thick batter. Let the dough age in a covered bowl in the refrigerator for about 3 days. Roll handfuls into long dowels on a floured cutting board. Cut into small pieces. Place pieces on greased and floured cookie sheets. Bake 350° for 8 minutes. Makes at least 5 dozen.

Chocolate Puppy Chow for Humans

A friend named Michele got this recipe from someone in her dog club.

- 1 (12-ounce) package milk chocolate chips
- 1 cup peanut butter, smooth
- 1 stick butter or margarine
- 1 (12.3-ounce) box Crispix cereal
- 2 cups confectioner's sugar

Place first 3 ingredients in a 3-quart saucepan and melt together over very low heat. When melted, pour over cereal in large bowl and stir until well coated. Pour mixture into a large brown paper grocery bag, add sugar and shake with the bag closed, until well mixed. Makes 10-12 servings.

Helaine's Brownies

Helaine is my favorite first cousin.

- 4 squares unsweetened baking chocolate
- 1/2 cup (1 stick) margarine or butter
- 2 cups sugar
- 4 eggs
- 1 cup flour
- 1 teaspoon vanilla
- 1 cup walnuts, chopped
- 1 cup chocolate chips

Melt chocolate and margarine or butter together over low heat in small saucepan (or in Pyrex measuring cup in microwave). Beat together sugar and eggs. Blend in chocolate mixture. Stir in flour and remaining three ingredients until well-mixed. Pour into greased 9" baking pan. Bake at 350° for 40 minutes. When cool cut into squares. Makes 12 servings.

Mandelbrot with Walnuts

This is a traditional Jewish cookie, but Moishe Rosen said it wasn't authentic because it included walnuts instead of almonds. Helaine (my cousin), lives in Sheepshead Bay in Brooklyn and is a very Jewish cook. We appeased Moishe by including her recipe and the one that follows it.

- 2 eggs
- 1/2 cup sugar
- 1 teaspoon vanilla
- 1/2 cup vegetable oil
- 2 cups flour

        1   teaspoon baking powder
             dash baking soda
             dash salt
       15   maraschino cherries, chopped
        1   cup mini chocolate chips (or regular)
      1/2   cup chopped walnuts
             cinnamon-sugar

Preheat oven to 350°. In large bowl, beat eggs, sugar and vanilla together until well blended. Add oil and mix. Add all dry ingredients. Add cherries, chocolate chips and walnuts. Blend well. Grease a cookie sheet with cooking spray or vegetable shortening. Put dough on greased sheet and, with wet hands, shape into a flat loaf. Sprinkle generously with cinnamon-sugar. Bake at 350° for 30 minutes. Slice into 1/4" thick slices when cool. Makes 2 dozen.

Mandelbrot with Almonds

        3   eggs
        1   cup sugar
      1/2   cup vegetable oil
      1/2   teaspoon almond extract
      1/2   teaspoon vanilla extracts
        2   tablespoons orange juice
             grated rind of 1 orange
        3   cups flour, sifted
        3   teaspoons baking powder
      1/4   teaspoon salt
   1 1/2   cups almonds, slivered

Beat eggs until thick and light. Add the sugar gradually, beating continuously. Add oil slowly, beating well. Add the extracts. Sift dry ingredients together; mix with nuts. Add to egg mixture, about a third at a time, mixing well. Knead on floured board for 10-12 turns. Divide the dough into several pieces and roll each piece into strips about 3" wide, 1" thick and 12" long. Place on shallow greased baking pan and bake at 350° until golden brown, about 35-45 minutes. Remove at once to cutting board; cut into 1/2" slices while still warm. Return to oven to brown slightly. Makes 3 dozen.

Lazy Lady Cookies

Line cookie sheet (one that has sides) with graham crackers, end to end. Put one stick margarine and one cup brown sugar in pan; cook and stir until sugar is dissolved and mixture is smooth and bubbly, about 3-5 minutes. Remove from stove and add 1 cup of chopped walnuts or pecans; mix well. Spread mixture on top of graham crackers (it will smooth out while baking). Bake at 350° for about 5 minutes, until bubbly. Let cool thoroughly; break into irregular pieces and watch them disappear! Makes about 2 dozen.

Lemon Bar Cookies

Hy Cohen's mother, Lil, gave us this recipe from her neighbor Ted.

1	stick butter or margarine
1/4	cup powdered sugar
1	cup flour
2	eggs
1	cup sugar
2 1/2	tablespoons flour
3	tablespoons lemon juice
1	teaspoon lemon rind, grated

Grease 8" square cake pan. Mix butter or margarine with powdered sugar and 1 cup flour. Spread evenly in pan and bake at 350° for 15-20 minutes. Whip together eggs, sugar, flour, lemon juice and rind. Pour on top of crust and bake 20 minutes. Let cool. Sprinkle powdered sugar on top. Cut into small squares. Makes 25 small or 16 large cookies.

Thick as a Fig Bars

1	cup brown sugar
1/2	cup oil
3	cup flour
1 1/2	cups instant rolled oats
1/2	teaspoon salt
2	eggs, beaten
1 1/2	cups dried figs, finely chopped

Cover figs with boiling water; leave overnight; drain before using. Combine sugar and oil in large bowl; beat until thick. Mix together flour, oats and salt in medium bowl. Add flour and eggs alternately to sugar/oil mixture. Mix until moist and spread half of mixture in lightly greased 8"x8" pan. Cover with plumped figs. Pour remaining batter over figs. Bake at 400° for 20-25 minutes. Cut into squares when cool. Makes 16 squares.

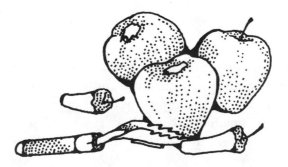

Is There Life After Dessert?

What can be said about dessert? Everybody loves it, but by the time you get around to eating it (especially if you cooked a meal from this cookbook) you're never really hungry enough to appreciate it fully. So maybe you should start a meal next time with dessert, as has been suggested by some wayward Jews for Jesus children.

A funny story (which has little to do with dessert) has traveled through the Jews for Jesus circles. One of our missionaries was in Israel a number of years ago. He had learned a few Hebrew words, and wanted to try them out. While in a restaurant, he summoned the waiter. "Adonai, Adonai," he motioned to the waiter. (This word actually means "Lord, Lord." He meant to say "Adoni, Adoni," which means "Mister, Mister"). The waiter, looking fairly amused, turned around and said, "What do you want to do, do you want to eat, or do you want to pray?"

As you can tell, this story has little to do with dessert, but perhaps you have ended up smiling. And that is as good an ending as anything else we could offer you.

Chocolate Mousse

2	teaspoons unflavored gelatin
1	can (15 ounces) sweetened, condensed milk
3	1-ounce squares unsweetened chocolate
3	eggs, separated
1	teaspoon vanilla extract
1/2	teaspoon rum extract

Soften gelatin in $1/4$ cup cold water in small bowl. In top of double boiler, over boiling water, combine milk and chocolate. Cook until chocolate melts. Continue cooking and stirring, until mixture is smooth and very thick, about 5 minutes. Gradually stir in 1/2 cup cold water. Keep stirring to keep mixture smooth. In small bowl, beat egg yolks slightly. Stir a small amount of the hot chocolate mixture into yolks. Add egg mixture to chocolate and return it to the top of the double boiler. Cook over hot water, stirring constantly until mixture is smooth and thick—about 5 minutes. Remove from heat and stir in softened gelatin, vanilla and rum extracts. Stir continuously until gelatin is dissolved. Cool to room temperature. Beat egg whites until they stand in stiff peaks. Test chocolate mixture to see if it will mound slightly when dropped from a spoon. When it does, fold in egg whites. Pour mixture into a 5-cup mold that has been lightly oiled. Refrigerate about 3 hours, or until firm. Makes 6 servings.

Easy Clean-Up Baked Custard

Custard can be a wonderfully easy dessert, but no one likes to clean the pan in which the milk is scalded. This recipe, which is about 20 years old, can be made in a blender without first scalding the milk.

2	cups milk
3	eggs
$1/3$	cup sugar
1	teaspoon vanilla extract
	pinch salt

Mix all ingredients in blender until well blended. Pour into lightly greased custard cups or small molds. Place these in a pan of hot water. Bake at 325° for 1 hour or until set. Makes 6 servings.

Absolutely Sublime Loaf

This recipe is a bit like Key Lime Pie.

Crust:
1	cup grated coconut
$1/4$	cup butter or margarine, softened
$1^{1}/_{2}$	cups vanilla cookie crumbs

Sauté the coconut in butter or margarine until golden brown, stirring constantly. Add cookie crumbs and mix well. Press into the bottom of a 9"x5" loaf pan or a 9" pie pan. Save 2-3 tablespoons of mixture to sprinkle over top.

Filling:
- 1　3-ounce package lime-flavored gelatin
- 1　cup boiling water
- 1¼　cups sugar
- 2　tablespoons lime or lemon juice
- 1　cup evaporated milk, chilled and whipped until thick

Dissolve gelatin in boiling water; stir in sugar and juice.
Chill until slightly thickened.
Fold in evaporated milk.
Put in crumb crust in pan.
Sprinkle reserved crumbs over top.
Chill well.
Makes 8 servings.

Rhubarb Crunch

Elaine Kvasnik from St. Paul, Minnesota gave us this recipe. She is barely 5' tall, but has a big heart for the Lord and is a real friend of Jews for Jesus. She also has 4 children and a big house to run, so I'm not sure when she finds the time to cook such delicacies as Rhubarb Crunch!

- 1　cup flour
- ¾　cup rolled oats
- 1　cup brown sugar
- ½　cup butter or margarine, melted
- 1　teaspoon cinnamon
- 4　cups sliced rhubarb
- 2　tablespoons cornstarch
- 1　teaspoon vanilla
- 1　cup sugar
- 1　cup water
- 　pinch salt

Mix flour, oats, sugar, butter and cinnamon together until crumbly.
Pat half of mixture into 9" baking dish.
Top with rhubarb.
Combine cornstarch, vanilla, sugar, water and salt in saucepan; cook and stir until thickened.
Pour cornstarch mixture over rhubarb; sprinkle with remainder of crumbs.
Bake at 350° for 1 hour.
Makes 6-8 servings.

A Persimmon Is Not a Tomato

A persimmon is not a tomato although it certainly resembles one. It is pinkish-orange when ripe, and differs from a tomato in its size and pointed stem end. Persimmons, when fully ripe and soft, need to be handled carefully and kept in the refrigerator. They can be eaten whole or used in recipes such as this one.

Sharon Hansen, from the Neighborhood Church in San Francisco, gave us this recipe.

1	cup flour, sifted
1/2	teaspoon salt
1/2	teaspoon baking soda
3/4	cup sugar
1	cup persimmon pulp (see preparation below)
2	eggs, beaten
1	cup milk
1/2	teaspoon lemon rind, grated
2	tablespoons butter or margarine

Prepare persimmon pulp: Choose soft, ripe fruit (you will need 2-3 persimmons) with transparent skins. Peel skin and discard seeds. Whip for a few seconds in food processor or blender. Sift together flour, salt, baking soda and sugar. Add persimmon pulp along with remaining ingredients. Mix well. Turn batter into greased and floured 8" square pan. Bake at 350° for 50 minutes or until set. Makes 6 servings.

Yennevelt Chocolate Eclair Dessert

This dessert was served to the New Jerusalem Players, a mobile evangelistic drama team of Jews for Jesus that traveled in the '70s. Nobody on the team at that time can remember where they ate this delicious dessert, or even who served it to them (shame on them!), but all will vouch for the fact that it is delicious. In case you're wondering, Yennevelt is a Yiddish word for "somewhere out there."

Line a 9"x13" pan with graham crackers (do not crush them). Mix 2 small packages instant vanilla pudding with 3 cups milk. Add 9 ounces frozen whipped topping, thawed. Spread this mixture over graham crackers; top with another layer of graham crackers. Spread with frosting: Melt together 2 squares unsweetened chocolate, 6 tablespoons butter or margarine, 3 tablespoons milk in small saucepan over low heat. Add 1 1/2 cups confectioner's sugar; beat together well. Makes 12 servings.

Peaches 'n Cream 'n Jello

A friend from Colorado made up this recipe, which is so easy it barely needs any explanation. Now there's no excuse for not making dessert.

1	(16-ounce) can sliced peaches
1	large box peach-flavored gelatin
1	package Dream Whip whipped topping mix

Drain liquid from peaches into measuring cup; add enough water to make 3 $\frac{1}{2}$ cups liquid. Prepare gelatin according to package directions, using peach liquid in place of water. Let mixture set in refrigerator, but do not let it gel completely. Beat with electric mixture until frothy; add prepared Dream Whip and whip well. Fold in cut-up peaches. Let set completely in refrigerator; arrange a few reserved sliced peaches over top to decorate, if desired. Makes 6 servings.

Depression Chocolate Pudding

During the '30s Depression everyone felt the pinch, and even simple desserts like chocolate pudding were considered a luxury. Winona Wellsfry's mother created this recipe at that time. It only calls for 5 $\frac{1}{2}$ tablespoons cocoa, but is certainly not short on taste.

1	cup flour
$\frac{3}{4}$	cup sugar
$1\frac{1}{2}$	tablespoons cocoa
2	tablespoons shortening
2	teaspoons baking powder
$\frac{1}{2}$	cup milk
$\frac{1}{2}$	teaspoon vanilla extract
$\frac{1}{2}$	cup walnuts, chopped
$\frac{1}{2}$	cup brown sugar
$\frac{1}{2}$	cup sugar
4	tablespoons cocoa

Mix first 8 ingredients together in 2-quart casserole. Cover with brown sugar/sugar/cocoa mixture. Pour 1 cup water over all and bake at 325° for 1 hour, or until set. Cool before serving. Makes 6 servings.

Thelma's Flan

$\frac{1}{2}$	cup sugar
1	cup water
1	(13-ounce) can evaporated milk
1	(14-ounce) can sweetened, condensed milk
1	(3-ounce) package cream cheese
4	eggs
1	tablespoon vanilla extract

Heat $\frac{1}{2}$ cup sugar with 1 cup water over medium heat, stirring constantly until thick and brown.
Pour into 8" casserole, turning to coat sides of pan.
Put remaining ingredients in blender; blend well on high speed.
Pour over sugar syrup in casserole.
Place pan in larger pan of hot water. Bake at 350° for 1 hour.
Makes 6 servings.

Hawaiian Pudding Cake

    3   tablespoons butter or margarine, softened
    2   cups sugar
    2   eggs
    2   cups crushed, canned pineapple (do not drain)
    2   cups flour
    1   teaspoon salt
    1   teaspoon baking soda
    1   teaspoon baking powder
    1/2 cup chopped pecans
         sweetened whipped cream
         crystallized ginger, chopped (for garnish)

Cream butter and sugar together; add eggs and crushed pineapple. Sift together flour, salt, baking soda and baking powder in separate bowl; add to creamed pineapple mixture. Beat all together well. Add chopped nuts. Pour into greased and floured 9"x13" baking dish. Bake at 350° for 45 minutes or until done (test as for a cake). Cut into squares when cool. Serve with sweetened whipped cream, to which has been added a little chopped crystallized ginger. Makes 10-12 servings.

Lime Sherbet Surprise

The surprise is that this dessert is so low in calories (only 80 per serving) that it barely deserves to be called dessert.

    1   (3-ounce) package lime-flavored gelatin
    1/2   cup sugar
    1 1/2 cups boiling water
    1   cup buttermilk
    1   teaspoon grated lemon or lime rind
    3   tablespoons lemon or lime juice
    1   egg white

In mixing bowl, combine gelatin and sugar; dissolve in boiling water. Stir in buttermilk, grated peel and juice. Put in a 4-cup refrigerator tray or dish; freeze until firm. Break up into chunks; with electric beater mix until smooth. Beat egg white until stiff peaks form. Fold into gelatin mixture. Spoon back into refrigerator tray; return to freezer until firm. Makes 10 1/2-cup servings.

Strawberry and Ricotta Tartletts

    1/2   cup ricotta cheese
    2   tablespoons honey
    1   pint strawberries, hulled, washed and sliced
    6-8   unsweetened tartlett shells, about 4" in diameter

In small bowl, blend together ricotta and honey. Fill shells about half full with ricotta mixture. Divide the sliced berries evenly amongst the shells. Makes 6-8 servings.

Chocolate Fondue

2 tablespoons honey
1/2 cup light cream or half-and-half
1 (8 3/4-ounce) bar milk chocolate, broken
1 teaspoon vanilla or mint extract

For dipping:
    pound cake or angel food cake chunks
    apple wedges
    sliced fresh pineapple
    banana chunks
    pitted cherries
    whole strawberries, hulled

Heat honey and cream together in fondue pot over a direct high flame. Lower heat and stir in chocolate pieces. Stir constantly until chocolate is melted. Add extract; stir. Serve with any of the listed dipping delights! Makes 4-6 servings.

Marcia's Fruit Compote

This compote is traditionally served at Passover but it is delicious anytime.

1 package each dried, pitted prunes and mixed dried fruit
1 box seedless raisins, can be mixed golden and dark
1 lemon, sliced
1/2 cup slivered almonds
    water to cover

Put all ingredients (except almonds) in saucepan; barely cover fruit with water. Bring to boil, lower heat and simmer, covered for 15 minutes. Add almonds; cook 10 minutes more or until fruit is soft. Makes 4-6 servings.

Vi's Greek Rice Pudding

There's rice pudding, and then there's rice pudding. This recipe is from a Greek friend, Vi Berger, who is married to Barry, a missionary to the Jewish people. Vi is Greek, and so is her rice pudding.

1/2 gallon milk, at room temperature
1 cup rice, raw
1 cup sugar
1 egg yolk
1/2 teaspoon vanilla extract

Place milk, rice and sugar in large saucepan; heat and stir until thick over low flame. Beat egg yolk with a little of the heated milk mixture and the vanilla extract. Add egg mixture to milk and rice in saucepan. Cook until well blended and thick. Cool. Makes 10-12 servings.

Macadamia Nut Truffles

Candy for dessert? Why not?

> 1   (12-ounce) package semisweet chocolate bits
> 3/4   cup condensed milk
> 1   teaspoon vanilla
> 1/3   cup cocoa
> 1   5-ounce can macadamia nuts, salted

In a heavy 2-quart saucepan over low heat, heat semisweet chocolate pieces until melted and smooth, stirring occasionally. Remove saucepan from heat (or place chocolate in medium bowl; cover with plate. Heat chocolate in microwave or MEDIUM about 5 minutes, or until melted. Watch carefully—chocolate burns easily in microwave). Stir in milk, vanilla and salt until well mixed. Refrigerate 1 hour. Divide chocolate mixture into 42 pieces. With hands dusted with cocoa, shape one piece of the chocolate mixture around a macadamia nut to form a ball. Roll ball lightly in cocoa. Repeat with remaining mixture and nuts. Store candies, refrigerated, up to two weeks. Makes 3 1/2 dozen candies (80 calories each).

Christina's Fudge

This recipe comes from Diane Cohen's beautiful and oldest granddaughter.

> 1   (12-ounce) package semisweet chocolate chips
> 1   stick butter
> 1   (16-ounce) box confectioner's sugar, sifted
> 2   eggs
> 2   teaspoons vanilla
> 3/4   cup walnuts or pecans, chopped
>   pinch salt

Melt chocolate chips and butter together in microwave until bubbly; remove. Let sit 5 minutes; stir.
Pour over remaining ingredients mixed together in large bowl. Beat like crazy! Pour into 9" greased pan.
Cut into small cubes when set. Makes 3 dozen.

Sarah's Grape Delight

The Jews for Jesus chief administrative officer Jonathan Markham's wife, Sarah, has delighted people on two continents with this creation.

> 1   bunch green grapes
>   brown sugar
> 1/2   pint cream
> 1/2   pint plain yogurt

Beat cream until stiff. Fold in yogurt. Add grapes. Immediately before serving sprinkle brown sugar over the mixture. Makes 6-8 servings.

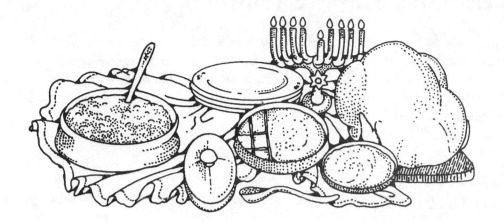

Holiday Recipes

Rosh Hashanah

Rosh Hashanah, the Jewish New Year, occurs in the early fall and marks the beginning of the High Holiday season. It takes place ten days before Yom Kippur and is celebrated for two days.

The special foods that are enjoyed at this time are symbolic of the hope for a sweet life in the New Year. Sliced apples are served with bowls of honey. Rabbinic tradition holds that the apple is a symbol of the Divine Presence. There is likely to be fresh challah to dip in the honey as well. This traditional braided Sabbath bread is baked in different shapes for Rosh Hashanah. A round challah symbolizes a crown. A ladder-shaped challah reminds us of Jacob's dream. A loaf can be baked in the shape of a bird, reminding us of God's hovering presence over us. Dried fruits and dishes prepared with dried fruits are also enjoyed, and it is traditional to eat dairy dishes.

Susan Perlman's Surprise Tzimmes

What's the surprise? Most people know Susan Perlman as first assistant to the executive director, Jews for Jesus media director, an international conference speaker and the competent, creative editor of ISSUES. So when could she ever have time to cook? That's the surprise! Susan has been known to make her delicious Passover tzimmes for special guests. And because she's so busy, those who sit around her table feel especially honored and blessed.

10	large carrots
10	medium potatoes
6	medium sweet potatoes
4	pounds beef brisket or chuck
1	medium onion, sliced thin
2	teaspoons salt
1/2	cup brown sugar
4	tablespoons flour
4	tablespoons melted chicken fat or margarine

Scrape and cut carrots into 2"-long pieces. Peel and cut potatoes into 1"-thick rounds and set aside in bowl of cold water. Sear the beef with the onion over high heat in a 5-quart Dutch oven or large pot. Turn the meat frequently until it is browned on all sides.

Add carrots to meat, water to cover, salt and brown sugar; bring to a boil. Reduce flame and cook over low heat for 2 hours. Drain potatoes and add to meat; continue cooking for 1 more hour, or until meat is tender. Liquid should be reduced by half at this point; if it reduces too quickly, add a little more water. Remove onion from pot. Pour contents into baking pan. Sauté flour in melted fat in a small saucepan; add 3 tablespoons of the tzimmes liquid to make a thickening agent. Mix this evenly throughout the baking pan. Sprinkle a little more brown sugar and cinnamon on top and bake in 350° oven for 30-40 minutes. Makes at least 12 servings.

Note: If this recipe is made for Passover, substitute matzoh meal for the flour.

Prunes and Potatoes

6	medium sized potatoes
1	pound pitted prunes
1	lemon, sliced thin
1	tablespoon salt
	chicken fat, butter or margarine
1	onion
1	tablespoon flour
1	tablespoon sugar

Peel and slice potatoes into thick slices. Wash prunes with hot water. Place part of the sliced potatoes in a well-greased casserole dish. Add a layer of prunes. Alternate until all the prunes and potatoes are used. Add sliced lemon over the top. Sprinkle with salt and pour in water to cover. Dot with chicken fat or butter or margarine. Add whole onion to casserole. Bake at 350° for $1/2$ hour; remove onion and bake another $1/2$ hour or until potatoes are tender. Mix flour with sugar; add enough cold water to make a smooth paste and pour into casserole. Continue baking until potatoes are lightly browned. Makes 8 servings.

Noodle Cheese Pudding

1	(16-ounce) package broad noodles
$1/2$	teaspoon salt
3	eggs
4	tablespoons butter or margarine
1	(8-ounce) package cream cheese
$1/2$	cup cottage cheese

Cook noodles according to package directions; drain. Add salt and eggs to noodles in large bowl; mix well. Heat butter or margarine in large frying pan; add half of the cooked noodles; then make a layer of each of the cheeses and cover with the rest of the noodles. Let pudding cook until brown over medium heat; then turn it over (like a huge pancake) and let cook until brown on other side. Makes 5-6 servings.

Taglach

6	eggs
3	cups flour
1	teaspoon cinnamon
2	teaspoons ginger
$1/4$	teaspoon salt
$1/4$	cup chopped walnuts
1/4	cup raisins
1 $1/2$	cups honey
3 $1/2$	cups brown sugar, packed

Beat eggs well and add flour, to which has been added cinnamon, one teaspoon of the ginger, salt, nuts and raisins. Make a soft dough of this mixture, just firm enough to be handled. Divide dough into six parts, rolling out each part with your hands into a long, thin roll about a $1/2$" thick in diameter; cut into $1/2$" pieces—they should be about the size of large marbles.

In a 5-quart saucepan or Dutch oven, cook together honey, sugar and remaining teaspoon ginger until blended. Bring to boiling, then drop in small pieces of dough one by one. Cover the saucepan; lower heat to continue boiling without scorching or boiling over. Shake the pan lightly from time to time to prevent the taglach from sticking to the pan.

Cook until pieces of dough are very brown and puffed. Remove pan from flame and add $1/2$ cup of boiling water. Be careful! The water causes the liquid to boil violently. Remove the taglach from the honey liquid and place on a large plate—and enjoy!

Authentic Jewish Bubba's Honey Cake

God bless our bubbas (grandmothers), and especially Joyce Weeks's Bubba Rose. Joyce is a Jews for Jesus Co-laborer in Minneapolis. When she heard we were putting together this cookbook, she immediately sent in her grandmother's recipe for this exceptional honey cake. It is now our pleasure to pass it on to you.

4	eggs
2	cups sugar
1	cup brown sugar, packed
1	16-ounces honey, slightly warmed (clover honey is good)
½	cup cold, strong coffee
1	cup peanut oil
1	teaspoon vanilla extract
5½	cups flour
2	teaspoons baking powder
2	teaspoons baking soda
2	teaspoons ground allspice
2	teaspoons cinnamon
2	oranges, grated (peel, pulp and all)
1	cup walnuts, chopped

Preheat oven to 350°. Beat eggs with both sugars. Add honey, brewed coffee, peanut oil and vanilla extract. In a separate bowl, sift flour with baking soda, baking powder and spices. Add grated orange to honey mixture; gradually beat in flour mixture. Add chopped nuts. Bake in 9x13" pan which has been lined with baker's parchment paper or brown paper bag cut to fit pan. Bake for 30 minutes or until cake tester inserted in center comes out clean. If cake starts to burn before done, cover top with brown paper and lower temperature by 25°. Makes 12-16 servings.

Prune-Nut Bars

1	cup flour
¾	cup sugar
¼	teaspoon salt
¼	teaspoon baking powder
½	cup applesauce
¼	cup water
2	eggs or egg substitute
½	teaspoon vanilla
½	teaspoon lemon rind, grated
1	cup walnuts or pecans, chopped
1	cup prunes, pitted and finely chopped

In large bowl, stir together flour, sugar, salt and baking powder. Make a well and add applesauce, water, eggs or egg substitute, vanilla and lemon rind. Add nuts and prunes and mix well. Spread in greased 9"x13" pan. Bake in 350° oven 35-40 minutes. Cut into bars while warm. Makes 32 bars.

Cheese Latkes

3	eggs, well beaten
1	cup milk
$\frac{1}{2}$	teaspoon cinnamon
1	tablespoon sugar
1	cup pot cheese or dry-curd cottage cheese
1	cup matzoh meal

Combine eggs, milk, cinnamon, sugar and cheese in a large bowl. Add matzoh meal until mixture is fairly dry. Drop by tablespoons onto a well-greased frying pan or griddle; brown on both sides. Serve with sour cream, applesauce or jelly. Makes approximately 16 pancakes.

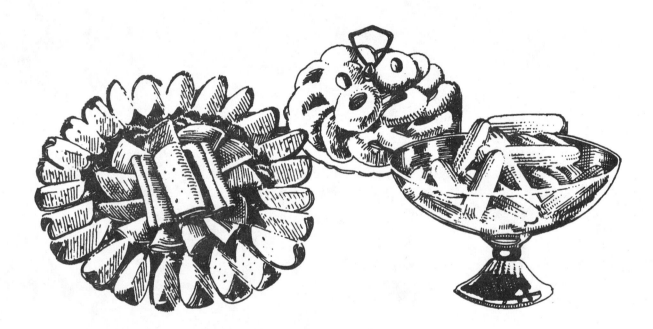

What to eat on Yom Kippur (Day of Atonement)

What to eat after Yom Kippur

No, the previous page isn't a printing error. During the fast day of Yom Kippur, observant Jews do just that—fast. The day is traditionally spent in the synagogue, praying and petitioning God for all the sins one has committed throughout the year. Jewish people all over the world view Yom Kippur as the most holy and solemn day of the year.

But thank God for Y'shua! Through Him we can come at any moment of the day to the Father's throne and confess our sins. Through His forgiveness and atoning work on the Cross we have been restored to a right relationship with God. We can enjoy the assurance that we are forgiven and know the pleasure of fellowship with Him.

You may want to identify with the Jewish people on this most holy day of the Jewish calendar, and observe the day through fasting and prayer, as well. If you do, let your prayers be praise for His mercy and petition for those who do not yet know Him. Pray on Yom Kippur that more of our people would find the true atonement and freedom of forgiveness through Christ.

If you decide to fast, fast as unto the Lord, and then break the fast by eating unto Him as well! A typical menu to break the fast might include chicken soup, roast chicken, a green vegetable, sweet potatoes and fruit compote. Or you might prefer a simpler meal of dairy dishes, such as cheese blintzes or kugel. Don't eat too much too soon, or you'll wish you hadn't. Recipes to break the fast can be found throughout this cookbook. Praise God for His Son, who promises us complete forgiveness and restoration if we put our faith and trust in Him.

Hanukkah

Hanukkah, the Feast of Dedication and the Festival of Lights, is not mentioned among the Old Testament feasts of Israel. However, it is mentioned in John 10:22. It is a time when Jewish people are reminded of their ancestors' fight for freedom more than 2,000 years ago. The story of Hanukkah goes like this: Around the year 175 b.c., a group of Jews, led by Judah Maccabee, revolted against the Syrian-Greek emperor, Antiochus IV. He had seized and desecrated the Temple in Jerusalem, filled it with idols and commanded the Jews to give up their faith. The three-year revolt, led by the Maccabees against Antiochus, was a victorious one. When the Jews returned to Jerusalem to cleanse the Temple, they rid it of its pagan objects and rededicated it to the worship of Jehovah.

The miracle of the Hanukkah story is found in this tale: Before the ark in the Temple a special "eternal light" was kept burning day and night—its light was never to go out. However, when Judah and his army arrived at the Temple they found only enough oil for the lamp to keep burning for one more day. Miraculously, the oil actually lasted eight days, and to this day, Jewish people all over the world celebrate Hanukkah, the Feast of Lights, for eight days. A special nine-candle hanukkiah (candelabra), one candle for each night of Hanukkah, is lit by a special shammas (helper) candle. Each night one more candle is lit, small gifts are given to the children, games are played, and of course, special foods are enjoyed.

It is customary at Hanukkah to eat foods that have been prepared with oil. And who can resist a platter of crisp, brown potato latkes (pancakes), served with homemade applesauce? Try the recipes included here, light your own menorah and celebrate that Y'shua is the light of the world.

A traditional Hanukkah dinner might include: chopped liver, raw vegetable crudites, mushroom barley soup, roast duck, string beans, potato latkes, fruit compote and Hanukkah cookies.

Award-Winning Potato Pancakes (Latkes)

I don't like to brag, but I did win first place for this recipe at a Hanukkah party held by the Chicagoland area Messianic community. What won the judges over? "We loved the onions," they said. Latkes are traditionally eaten with homemade applesauce or sour cream, but for some reason, my husband Jhan always eats his with catsup.

4	large potatoes, scrubbed and left unpeeled
1	medium onion
3	small eggs or egg substitute
$1/3$	cup flour (for Passover these can be made with $1/4$ cup matzoh meal)
	salt and pepper to taste
	vegetable oil
	applesauce or sour cream (or catsup)

Grate potatoes with the onion, either by hand (if you have the energy and the knuckles!) or in the food processor, using the steel blade. You should have a mixture the consistency of coarsely chopped apples for applesauce. Place potatoes and onions in colander to drain over sink. When drained, put mixture in large bowl and mix in eggs and flour (or matzoh meal). Season with salt and pepper. Pour vegetable oil to $1/4$ " depth in heavy skillet. Heat until very hot, but not smoking. Spoon batter into skillet, flattening pancakes into 3" ovals. Fry until deep golden brown and crisp on both sides. Repeat with all the mixture. Lay several newspapers on kitchen counter; cover with several paper towels and place cooked pancakes on this to drain. Serve immediately or if you have to, keep warm in a 400° oven (they will lose some of their crispness, but will taste just as good). Makes 24 latkes. Serve with applesauce or sour cream (or catsup).

Potato Latkes

1	pound potatoes, grated with peel left on
2	eggs, beaten
2-4	tablespoons flour or matzoh meal
$1/4$	teaspoon baking powder
$1\,1/2$	teaspoons salt
$1/4$	teaspoon pepper
2	tablespoons finely grated onion
1	teaspoon lemon juice
	oil for frying

After grating potatoes, drain in large colander.

When well-drained, pour into bowl with remaining ingredients and mix all together until well-blended (the amount of flour or matzoh meal you use depends on how watery the potato mixture is).

Add 1/4" layer of oil to a large frying pan and heat over medium heat.

Shape potato mixture into small, oval pancakes, about 3"x4".

Fry pancakes over medium heat for approximately 5 minutes on each side, until golden brown.

Makes 12 latkes.

Homemade Applesauce

Peel, core and coarsely chop 3 pounds of apples (any kind except Delicious).

Place in large pot and add about 2" of water.

Cover and let apples cook over low heat until very soft and mushy—can be pressed down with potato masher or large spoon.

More water can be added if necessary, but the water released from the apples should be sufficient.

A small amount of sugar or honey can be used to sweeten the applesauce, if desired.

Sprinkle with cinnamon or nutmeg to taste.

Serve warm or cold.

Fruit Fritters

1/2	cup flour
1/2	cup whole wheat pastry flour
	pinch salt
2	tablespoons sugar or 1 tablespoon honey
1	egg, beaten
2	tablespoons butter or margarine, melted
	oil for deep-fat frying
	fresh fruit: 2 bananas, thickly sliced OR 3-4 apples, cored and thickly sliced OR 12 thin slices fresh pineapple OR 3-4 peaches, thickly sliced OR 2 large pears, thickly sliced

Mix all ingredients except oil and fruit, to make a batter thick enough to coat the fruit.

Blend until smooth, but do not overbeat.

Drop pieces of fruit into the batter, letting excess drain off slightly.

Deep fry at 375° until batter is well-browned and fruit is tender when pierced with fork.

Drain on paper towels and sprinkle lightly with confectioner's sugar.

Makes 4-6 servings.

Hanukkah Cookies

1	cup butter or margarine
3/4	cup sugar or 1/2 cup honey
2	eggs
1 1/2	cups flour
1/2	cup whole wheat flour or whole wheat pastry flour
1/4	teaspoon salt
1/2	teaspoon baking powder
1	teaspoon vanilla, almond or orange extract

Cream butter or margarine together with sugar or honey.

Beat in eggs and mix together well.

Add dry ingredients (which have been sifted together), then extract.

Form dough into a ball; chill in refrigerator at least 1 hour before rolling out.

Roll out 1/8" thick on floured board; cut into shapes using holiday cookie cutters (in the shape of menorahs, dreidels or Jewish stars).

Bake at 375° for 8-10 minutes on ungreased cookie sheets; let cool on wire rack.

Can be decorated with blue icing, if desired.

Makes 4 dozen.

Fruit Compote

1/2	pound each dried apricots, peaches and pears, soaked overnight in water to cover
2	oranges
1/8	teaspoon ground allspice
1/4	cup honey
1/8	cup sugar

Drain liquid from fruit; reserve.

Over a bowl, remove rind from oranges and grate rind (only the orange part) finely; reserve juice.

Add rind to reserved liquid from dried fruits, along with the juice from the oranges, allspice, honey, and half the sugar.

Bring gently to a boil and simmer until thick.

Pour over fruit. Chill until serving time.

Makes 8-10 servings.

Purim

For Jewish boys and girls, Purim means dressing up and eating hamantaschen. It is a holiday of merriment and remembrance. Through her faithfulness, Esther, a young Jewish maiden, was elevated to the position of princess and deliverer of her people. The story is told in the Book of Esther, and each year the entire book is read during the holiday celebration. Groggers, or noisemakers, are shaken and twirled whenever the wicked Haman's name is read, and boo's and foot stomping are in order.

This holiday would not be complete without hamantaschen, 3-cornered cakes shaped to resemble Haman's (boo!) hat.

Hamantaschen

Dough:
3/4	cup vegetable oil
1	cup sugar
3	eggs
1/2	cup liquid from prunes (see prune filling below)
4³/4	cups flour
2	teaspoons baking powder
1/2	teaspoon salt

In large bowl, mix together oil, sugar, eggs and liquid from the prunes until well-blended. Sift together dry ingredients and add to this mixture. Blend dough together well and refrigerate, covered, for at least 1 hour.

Remove dough from refrigerator. Divide dough into 3 parts. Roll each piece out to 1/4" thick on well-floured board. Cut out 3" rounds. Put 1/2 tablespoon filling on each round. Fold 3 sides up to the center and pinch edges together to shape a 3-cornered hat with a hole in the middle to show the filling.

Bake on a greased baking sheet, slightly apart, at 375° about 12 minutes, or until golden brown.

Prune filling:
12	ounces pitted prunes
2	lemons, sliced
	boiling water to cover prunes
1/2	cup walnuts, finely chopped
1	apple, peeled and finely chopped
1/4	cup honey or 1/2 cup sugar
1	teaspoon cinnamon

Cover prunes and lemon with boiling water. Let stand 1/2 hour or bring to a boil and simmer 10 minutes. Drain juice and reserve. Put all filling ingredients in food processor and process until well-mixed.

Poppyseed filling:

1/2	cup	water
1/2	cup	sugar
3/4	cup	poppy seeds
1/4	cup	fine bread crumbs
2-3	tablespoons	honey
3	tablespoons	lemon juice
1	teaspoon	grated lemon rind

Bring the water and sugar to boil in heavy saucepan. Lower the heat, add the poppy seeds and cook, stirring until the mixture thickens. Stir in the remaining ingredients and remove from heat.

Date filling:

4	cups	dates
3	tablespoons	margarine
2	teaspoons	cinnamon
2/3	cup	water
1/2	cup	sugar
1	cup	walnuts or almonds, chopped

Place all ingredients except nuts in heavy saucepan and bring to boil over medium heat. Lower heat and cook 8-10 minutes until mixture is heavy and thick. Add nuts and remove from heat.

Passover

Passover! The mere thought of this joyous Festival of Redemption delights the soul, both Jewish and Gentile. Each spring, Jewish men, women and children prepare their hearts and their homes in anticipation of the holiday. It is a feast of remembrance, a time to thank God for His deliverance of the ancient Israelites from Egyptian bondage. For Jewish and Gentile believers, who know the true Redeemer of Israel, the Messiah Jesus, Passover has additional significance. It is a time of gratitude for God's total redemption and deliverance of mankind from the bondage of sin.

For Jew or Gentile, Passover always means a feast. And you don't have to be Jewish to prepare the special dishes eaten at this time. All you need are some measuring spoons, a few ingredients found in most major supermarkets during the Passover season, and these recipes. Compiled here are traditional recipes, all bearing the Jews for Jesus Good Foods Seal of Approval. (Next to handing out our Gospel tracts, eating is our favorite pastime!).

So go ahead and enjoy! Many of the recipes make 8 to 12 servings, so be sure to invite a big group. Insist that everyone bring a big appetite. May God inhabit your home as you enjoy and worship Him, the true Atonement, the Paschal Lamb of God.

Note: For additional Passover recipes refer to the booklet Passover Recipes *by Melissa Moskowitz (Purple Pomegranate Productions).*

Appetizers

Gefilte Fish

3	pounds whitefish
2½	pounds pike
½	pound carp
4	large onions
2	quarts water
4	teaspoons salt
1½	teaspoons pepper
3	eggs
¾	cup ice water
1	teaspoon sugar
3	tablespoons matzoh meal
3	carrots, sliced into ¼ ″ rounds, sliced

Fillet the fish (or have the fishmonger fillet it for you); reserve the head, skin and bones. Combine the head, skin and bones with 3 sliced onions, 1 quart water, 2 teaspoons salt and ¾ teaspoon pepper. Bring to a rapid boil, lower heat slightly and keep boiling while preparing fish.

Grind or chop fish finely (or have it ground for you) with remaining onion. Place in a chopping bowl and add the eggs, ice water, sugar, matzoh meal and remaining salt and pepper. Continue chopping until very fine. Moisten hands; shape mixture into slightly flattened loaves approximately 3"x2"x1". Carefully drop loaves into fish stock. Add 3 sliced carrots, cover loosely and cook over low heat for 1 ½ hours. Remove cover and cook for ½ hour more. Cool fish slightly before removing to serving platter. Strain the stock over the fish and arrange cooked carrots around it. Serve with horseradish. Makes 12 servings.

Chopped Liver

1	pound chicken livers, washed and drained
3	medium onions, chopped
1	clove garlic, mashed
¼	cup oil
2	hard-cooked eggs
1	teaspoon salt
	pepper

Dry the chicken livers with paper towels. Sauté the onions and mashed garlic in oil until brown. Remove from pan and add chicken livers. Cook until they have lost their red color. Turn heat down to medium and simmer for 10 minutes. Remove from heat. Put all ingredients in food processor or blender in 2 batches. Blend until mixture resembles a fine paste. Correct seasoning, if necessary. Serve in small scoops on lettuce leaves as a first course or as a spread for matzohs. Serves at least 12 as a spread, or 6 as a first course.

Knaidlach #1 (Matzoh Balls) for Soup

6   eggs, separated
1   teaspoon salt
1/8 teaspoon pepper
2   tablespoons melted chicken fat or margarine
1   cup matzoh meal

Beat egg whites until stiff. Beat egg yolks separately until light. Add salt, pepper and melted fat to yolks; fold gently into egg whites. Fold in matzoh meal 1 spoonful at a time. Refrigerate for at least 1 hour. Moisten hands and form batter into walnut-sized balls. Drop into large pot of rapidly boiling chicken soup or water. Reduce heat and cook slowly, covered, for 30 minutes. Makes 12 servings.

Charoseth

2   tart apples
1/2 cup walnuts
1/4 teaspoon cinnamon
1   teaspoon honey
1   tablespoon sweet Passover wine

Core apples (it is not necessary to peel them). Chop apples and walnuts together in food processor or blender, or chop by hand until finely chopped. With a wooden spoon, stir in cinnamon, honey and wine to make a thick, chunky paste. Will serve 10-12 people, with 1 teaspoon to 1 tablespoon apiece.

Beet Borscht

2   quarts hot water
6   beets with tops
1/4 teaspoon salt
1   cup sugar
4   tablespoons lemon juice
1   cup sour cream
4   small boiled potatoes, cold

Wash beets and beet tops well; peel beets. Slice beets into a large saucepan; add hot water and chopped beet tops. Add sugar, salt and lemon juice. Boil 10 minutes, skim liquid, lower heat and simmer 1/2 hour or until beets are cooked. Serve hot in bowls with round tablespoon of sour cream and a boiled potato on top of each serving. Makes 4 servings.

Main Dishes

Moishe's Roast Lamb for Passover

Have butcher bone and roll a lamb shoulder or leg—figure on $1/2$-$3/4$ pound boned and rolled lamb per person. You will need 2 cloves of garlic for every 1 pound of lamb. Slice garlic into thin slices; make holes with the point of a sharp knife in the fatty part of the lamb. Insert slices of garlic into holes. Place meat thermometer in the center of the thickest part of the lamb. Roast at 325° on a rack in a shallow pan until meat thermometer reaches 175° (medium done) or 180° (well done)—about 35-40 minutes per pound.

Matzoh Farfel Stuffing

$1/2$	cup ice water
3 $1/2$	cups matzoh farfel (or crumbled matzohs)
3	eggs
1	teaspoon salt
4	tablespoons melted margarine or chicken fat
1	finely chopped onion
1	cup prunes, finely chopped and pitted
2	tablespoons sugar
	pinch cinnamon

Sprinkle matzoh farfel or crumbled matzohs with ice water. In a large bowl, beat eggs and add the moistened matzoh and salt. Sauté chopped onion in melted fat until light brown and add this to matzoh mixture. Let cool. Add prunes, cinnamon and sugar. Put mixture back in frying pan and cook over moderate heat, stirring, until excess moisture has evaporated. Let cool before stuffing bird in usual manner. Stuffs a 4 $1/2$-5 pound chicken; can be doubled for larger bird.

Matzoh Stuffing

4	matzohs, broken into bite-size pieces
	ice water to cover matzohs
1	teaspoon salt
3	eggs, beaten
1	onion, finely chopped
$1/2$	cup celery, finely chopped
1	green pepper, chopped
3	tablespoons margarine or chicken fat

In a deep bowl, cover broken matzohs with ice water and let stand 5 minutes. Squeeze dry and put in mixing bowl. Add beaten eggs and salt to moist matzohs. Cook onion, celery and green pepper until soft in melted fat; add to matzoh mixture. Stuffs an average-sized fowl (about a 5-pound chicken). Mixture can be doubled to stuff a larger bird.

A Few Extras

Passover Blintzes

Blintze wrappers:
- 8 ounces potato flour
- 2 eggs
- 1½-2 cups ice water
- Vegetable oil or cooking spray

Put the potato flour in a large bowl. Make a well in the center and break the eggs in it. Mix into a thin batter with ice water. Heat a small frying pan after lightly greasing it with oil or cooking spray. Pour in sufficient batter to make a thin pancake, tilting pan so that the entire surface is covered. Cook on one side only until the pancake is set; continue until all the batter is used. Flip out of pan, cooked side up, onto sheet of waxed paper. Put in heaping tablespoon of filling; fold in sides of wrapper; fry in oil until lightly browned on both sides.

Cheese filling:
- ½ pound dry-curd cottage cheese (or pot cheese)
- 1 egg
- 1 tablespoon sugar
- 1 tablespoon sour cream
- ⅛ cup melted butter or margarine
- ¼ teaspoon salt
- ½ teaspoon lemon juice

Meat filling:
- 1 cup ground beef browned with ½ onion, minced
          OR
- 1 cup leftover cooked chicken or beef sautéed with ½ onion, minced
- ½ tablespoon melted chicken fat or margarine
- 1 egg, beaten
- salt and pepper to taste

Combine all ingredients for either cheese or meat blintzes (or make both!) and fill blintze wrappers as indicated. Makes 6 servings.

Matzoh Brie

Cecilia Butcher suggests that you offer maple syrup along with this dish.

2   matzohs, broken into bite-size pieces
    hot water
2   eggs, beaten
    salt and pepper to taste
2   tablespoons margarine or butter

Put broken matzohs in colander; run hot water over them until slightly softened. Squeeze matzohs dry. Beat eggs, salt and pepper in large bowl; add drained matzohs and mix well. Melt butter or margarine in large skillet; add matzoh/egg mixture. Cover and cook over moderate heat until lightly browned; turn and brown other side, breaking up matzohs with a wooden spoon or spatula. Makes 2 servings.

Matzoh Pancakes

1/2   cup matzoh meal
  3   tablespoons melted margarine or butter
  1   tablespoon water
  3   eggs, beaten
      salt and pepper to taste

Combine all ingredients except melted fat and let stand for an hour in the refrigerator. Heat fat in large frying pan; drop mixture by large tablespoons and brown on both sides. Drain on paper towels. Serve with applesauce or sour cream. Makes 10-12 pancakes.

Matzoh Kugel with Cheese

4-6   matzohs
  4   eggs
  1   cup milk
  1   pound cottage cheese
1/2   teaspoon salt
  2   teaspoons brown sugar
1/4   teaspoon cinnamon
  2   tablespoons margarine or butter

Break matzohs into 2" pieces. Mix eggs with milk and reserve 1/2 cup of mixture. Mix remaining egg/milk mixture with the cottage cheese, salt, brown sugar and cinnamon. Dip the matzoh into the reserved egg-milk mixture. Arrange these in layers in a greased 3-quart baking dish. Dot each layer with butter or margarine and the prepared cheese. The last layer should be matzoh covered with any remaining milk/egg mixture. Bake at 350° for 35-40 minutes. Makes 4-6 servings.

Desserts

Passover Cake

11	egg whites
11	egg yolks, well-beaten
2	cups sugar
4	cups hazelnuts, ground
4	tablespoons matzoh meal
1	tablespoon (heaping) potato starch

Beat egg whites until stiff. In separate bowl, beat together egg yolks, sugar, hazelnuts, matzoh meal and potato starch. Gently fold in egg whites. Grease a 10" springform pan very well; sprinkle with matzoh meal. Slowly pour cake batter into prepared pan. Bake at 350° for 1 hour. Cool completely before removing from pan. Makes 8-12 servings.

Almond Macaroons

1	pound blanched almonds, finely chopped
5	egg whites
1 1/2	pounds confectioner's sugar
5	tablespoons matzoh cake meal
	grated rind of one lemon

Beat egg whites until stiff (but not dry); add sugar a little at a time until it is all blended in. Fold in cake meal, lemon rind and ground almonds, being careful not to break down the egg whites. Drop from a teaspoon onto a foil-lined cookie sheet, leaving 1" between drops. Bake at 300° for 15-18 minutes or until lightly browned on top and bottom. Let cool; peel off foil. Makes approximately 3-3 1/2 dozen macaroons.

Passover Nut Cake

8	eggs, separated and at room temperature
8	tablespoons sugar
1/2	teaspoon grated lemon rind
1	tablespoon lemon juice
2	tablespoons matzoh cake meal
1	cup almonds or pecans, finely ground

Beat egg yolks until light and lemon-colored; add sugar gradually and continue to beat until well-blended. Blend in lemon rind, juice, matzoh meal and ground nuts until well-mixed. Beat egg whites until stiff and blend in gently. Bake in an ungreased 10" springform pan for 1 hour at 300° or until the cake springs back when pressed lightly in the middle. Invert pan on cake rack to cool. Remove from pan when cool.

A Short Chapter of Treif–or, Thank God, Y'shua Made us Kosher

Moishe Rosen wanted me to set aside all the recipes that contain treif, or non-kosher (unclean) ingredients, and put them together in one chapter. We don't believe food can make a person righteous or unrighteous before God, but we do know that many of our Jewish brethren follow the Old Testament injunction against eating certain types of food. Therefore, we wanted to give you the option to partake or not, knowing that it is only the blood of our Messiah that makes us clean before God.

Cinesi's Gravy

Susan and Donald Cinesi are good New York friends of some of the original Jews for Jesus. When Susan (who is Jewish) married Donald (who is Italian), she quickly learned what is really important to an Italian husband: good gravy (we know it as spaghetti sauce).

1	large onion	2	links hot Italian sausage
1	tablespoon olive oil		
3	cloves garlic, crushed	³/₄	pound ground beef
1	(28-ounce) can plum tomatoes	¹/₄	pound ground pork
	(preferably an Italian brand)	1	egg
3	ounces tomato paste	¹/₂	cup grated
	salt and pepper to taste		Romano cheese
	dried basil		bread crumbs
	dried parsley	¹/₂	medium onion,
	dried oregano		finely chopped
6-8	links sweet Italian sausage	2	cloves garlic, crushed

Chop onion coarsely; brown lightly in one tablespoon olive oil in a large pot. Add crushed garlic to onions in pot and brown lightly. Add plum tomatoes (undrained), tomato paste, salt and pepper to taste, 2 tablespoons dried parsley, 2 teaspoons dried oregano, and 2 teaspoons dried basil.

In frying pan, brown both types of sausages, breaking up sausage as it cooks. When brown, drain and add to sauce.

In large bowl, mix together ground beef, ground pork, egg, Romano, bread crumbs, 1 tablespoon dried parsley, ¹/₂ teaspoon dried basil, ¹/₂ teaspoon dried oregano, salt and pepper to taste. Brown ¹/₂ chopped onion and two crushed garlic cloves in frying pan; add to ground meat mixture. Form into balls the size of small walnuts; the consistency should be of wet dough. Add to sauce. Bring sauce to a boil over medium heat; lower heat and simmer, covered, over low heat for 2-3 hours (stirring occasionally so that sauce doesn't stick to the bottom of the pot). Makes enough for 1 pound of pasta, to serve 4-6.

Note: Amounts of ingredients can be increased to suit your needs.

Caesar Salad

This recipe was submitted by Cecilia Butcher, another great Jews for Jesus campaign cook. Mrs. Butcher is the head of our Co-Laborers in Messiah program at our San Francisco headquarters office and is known to be willing to serve a meal to anyone who needs it. This recipe comes from an old friend of Cecilia's, who owns a restaurant in Seattle.

Croutons:
- ¹/₂ loaf day-old French or Italian bread
- 2 tablespoons olive oil

Cut bread into bite-size cubes. Heat oil in large frying pan and sauté bread cubes until golden. Drain on paper towels and set aside. Pour off oil and cook:

2 strips bacon

Fry until crisp. Crumble and set aside.

Dressing:
$1/4$ cup olive oil
$1/2$ cup lemon juice (fresh is best)
1 teaspoon Worcestershire sauce
anchovy paste, 1"-2"
salt and pepper

Mix all together well in jar and set aside.

1 large head romaine lettuce
1-2 tomatoes
1 coddled egg
$1/4$-$1/2$ cup Parmesan cheese, grated

Tear lettuce leaves into bite-sized bits. Place them in large salad bowl that's been rubbed with 1 clove cut garlic. Toss lettuce with tomatoes, cut into bite-size pieces. Pour in dressing, toss; add crumbled bacon, Parmesan cheese and coddled egg. Toss gently and serve immediately. Makes 6-8 servings.

Layered Salad

This salad looks particularly impressive when served in a pretty glass bowl. If you're like most of us, however, who do not own such an item, the salad tastes equally delicious when served from a plain, plastic bowl.

4 slices bacon, fried
(drain, crumble and set aside)
1 small head lettuce, chopped
1 red onion, thinly sliced
2 stalks celery, thinly sliced
3 radishes, thinly sliced
2 hard-boiled eggs, thinly sliced
1 cup frozen petite peas, thawed

$1^{1}/4$ cups mayonnaise
1 tablespoon lemon juice
salt and pepper
garlic powder
$1/2$ cup cheddar cheese, shredded

Place chopped lettuce in a layer in the bottom of a large bowl. Over this layer red onion, then chopped celery, sliced radishes, sliced hard-boiled eggs and thawed peas. Mix mayonnaise together with lemon juice, salt, pepper and garlic powder to taste; spread over top of layered vegetables. Sprinkle with shredded cheddar and crumbled bacon. Cover bowl with plastic wrap and refrigerate several hours before serving. Makes 8 servings.

Anna's Clam Chowder

Drain one 6 $\frac{1}{2}$-ounce can minced clams; reserve liquid, set aside. Finely chop $\frac{1}{4}$ pound salt pork; sauté in frying pan until golden. Add 1 large or 2 medium chopped onions; sauté until glossy. Add 3 to 4 cups of cubed, peeled raw potatoes and 1-1$\frac{1}{2}$ cups of boiling water, salt and pepper to taste.

Simmer until potatoes are just tender.

Add 1 small can evaporated milk plus enough fresh milk to make one pint.

Melt 1 tablespoon butter and 1 tablespoon flour; add reserved clam juice and cook to thicken; add to soup. Taste and adjust seasoning if needed. A little bottled clam juice can be added for more taste.

Anna's Lentil Soup

Sort and wash 1 pound of lentils. Add:

In a large pot combine lentils with 8 cups water, 2 medium onions, chopped, 2 carrots, chopped, 1 cup celery, chopped, 2 bay leaves, 1 ham bone, $\frac{1}{2}$ teaspoon pepper, $\frac{1}{2}$ teaspoon dried thyme, 2 tablespoons lemon juice and 2 cups diced potatoes. Bring to a boil, lower heat and cook, covered, until potatoes and lentils are soft (about 25 minutes); add salt to taste, and garlic powder.

Note: This can be made with beef stock instead of water. Just before potatoes are done, you can add a few pieces of smoked sausage. Onions can also be sautéed in a little butter before they are added to the soup.

Non-Bratty Brats

This recipe is from Judy Gartman, who says that her father-in-law in Wisconsin often makes this dish for family gatherings. You can substitute kosher beef franks for the bratwurst (in which case this recipe would no longer be considered treif), or even Italian sausages, if you prefer.

1	(16-ounce) can sauerkraut
10	ounces apple juice
$\frac{1}{4}$	cup sugar
$\frac{1}{2}$	teaspoon caraway seeds
6-8	bratwurst

Cook bratwurst in covered pan with a little water for 15 minutes. Drain. Combine all ingredients in a large saucepan and cook, covered, for 1 hour (in a crockpot, cook 4-5 hours on low setting). Serve bratwurst in hot dog buns and be sure to include the sauerkraut! Makes 6 servings.

Moishe Rosen's Famous Chili

You now know what all Jews for Jesus staff members know—that Moishe Rosen makes some of the best chili this side of heaven. Not only is the chili delicious, but Moishe takes a tremendous amount of pleasure in preparing it. And the staff takes a tremendous amount of pleasure in eating it!

- 2   pounds pinto beans, soaked overnight with 1 teaspoon garlic salt added to the water
- 2   pounds beef chorizo
- 1   pound tenderized round steak, diced small
- 1   can (28-ounce) stewed tomatoes or tomato sauce
- 6   tablespoons chili powder
- 3   onions, minced
- 2   bell peppers, chopped

Cook pinto beans until soft/firm; drain.
Squeeze chorizo out of its casing; brown in large frying pan.
Brown round steak in same pan.
In large pot, place meat, vegetables and chili powder; simmer 20 minutes.
Mix in beans and let simmer another 15 minutes. Makes 10 servings.

Optional: Add 1 crushed clove garlic for every $\frac{1}{2}$ pound meat.

Conclusion

Cookbooks don't usually have conclusions. An index should be enough. After all, cookbooks are written to be consulted, not read. But in closing, I wanted to ask a question and I hope you don't mind. My question is not what you think of my recipes, but, rather, what do you think of Y'shua? After all, you can eat well even if you don't know about my recipe book, but you can't live well if you don't know the Savior. So indulge me a little bit, and let me explain how you can know Him:

1. Realize that God is concerned with every aspect of your life.

"Can a woman forget her nursing child,
And not have compassion on the son of her womb?
Surely they may forget,
Yet I will not forget you.
See, I have inscribed you on the palms of My hands."   (Isaiah 49:15,16)

2. Acknowledge that you can't truly experience God's love because of sin.

"But your iniquities have separated
you from your God.
And your sins have hidden His face from you
So that He will not hear."   (Isaiah 59:2)

3. Trust in God's provision of Y'shua (Jesus) to be your sin-bearer and Savior.

"But He was wounded for our transgressions,
He was bruised for our iniquities;
The chastisement for our peace was upon Him,
And by His stripes we are healed."   (Isaiah 53:5)

"But God demonstrates His own love toward us,
in that while we were still sinners, Christ died for us."   (Romans 5:8)

4. Receive forgiveness of sins and a personal relationship with God by asking Y'shua to reign in your heart.

". . .If you confess with your mouth the Lord Jesus, and believe in your heart that God has raised Him from the dead, you will be saved. For with the heart one believes unto righteousness, and with the mouth confession is made unto salvation."   (Romans 10:9, 10)

Is there any good reason why you cannot receive Y'shua right now?

What to pray:

God of Abraham, I know that I have sinned against you, and I want to turn from my sins. I believe you provided Y'shua as a once and for all atonement for me. With this prayer, I receive Y'shua as my Savior and my Lord. I thank you for cleansing me of sin and making me worthy of the life you have for me through Messiah. Amen.

Index

Notes and Your Recipes:

Fig Bars   pg 144
Vinegar Pastry 135
Italian Pound Cake pg 126
Viv's Baklava Rolls pg 124
Baklava   pg 123
Yummy Coffee Cake pg 118
Garlic Butter pg 116
Leah's Pizza pg 114
Lowfat Fruit 'nd Bran Muffins pg 112
Real Rye Bread pg 106
Rice Tuna Bake pg 100
Chinese Rice pg 100
Baked Beans from Abuquerque pg 99
Potatoe Pancakes pg 92
Mc Hugh's Noodle Kugel (Pudding) pg 88
Grandma Broom's Homemade Noodles pg 85
Sauerkraut to Convince You pg 77
Savery Spinach pg 76
Orange Glazed Duck pg 64
Lamb Shanks pg 50
Anna's Onion Soup pg 30